SEX AND BACON

WHY I LOVE THINGS THAT ARE VERY, VERY BAD FOR ME

Sarah
Katherine
Lewis

SEAL PRESS

SEX AND BACON
WHY I LOVE THINGS THAT ARE VERY, VERY BAD FOR ME

Published by
Seal Press
A Member of Perseus Books Group
1700 Fourth Street
Berkeley, California 94710

Library of Congress Cataloging-in-Publication Data

Lewis, Sarah Katherine.
  Sex and bacon : why I love things that are very, very bad for me / by Sarah Katherine Lewis.
     p. cm.
  ISBN-13: 978-1-58005-228-3
  ISBN-10: 1-58005-228-2
  1. Vices. 2. Pleasure—Social aspects. I. Title.
  BJ1534.L49 2008
  394.1'2—dc22
                          2008004011

Cover and interior design by Domini Dragoone
Interior photographs © www.123rf.com
Printed in the United States of America
Distributed by Publishers Group West

To the ladies and gentlemen who have shared my bed and eaten my food, especially those of you who arrived with bags of groceries and stayed to wash dishes.

CONTENTS

III. SWEET

Fried Chicken Interlude: Chicken Bus

IV. PAIN

AFTERWORD: CHERRY ON TOP

I.
DESIRE

INTRODUCTION

I told you from the start just how this would end
When I get what I want I never want it again —Hole

I was out dancing last night with a pack of dear friends. A stranger approached our table preceded by the eye-watering aroma of gin and tobacco imperfectly filtered through skin. He finished his drink with a flourish and slammed his empty glass onto our table.

"You're pretty hot, baby," he slurred, breathing hot juniper fumes into my face. "Did those tattoos hurt?"

"My guess is you're pretty drunk," I said. My friend Jessica tittered.

He ignored my assessment, swaying in his shoes. "You're hot," he repeated. "I'm going to buy you a drink."

"No, thank you," I said. "I have one."

"I'm going to buy you another of the same—what is it?"

"I'd prefer you didn't, but thank you just the same."

The men—my friends—at the table glanced at each other, unsure whether to intervene.

I maintained level eye contact with the stranger. "See you later," I said.

In a flash the stranger's smile turned sour. "You're a *bitch*," he said. Snatching his empty glass protectively, he stomped away from our table. "Freaky bitch," he muttered.

My eyes met Jessica's for a moment. I shrugged. *Could have been worse.*

She nodded.

Both of us knew that could have gotten ugly. We were grateful it hadn't, and that our sweet male friends hadn't been forced to act *in loco boyfriendis* out of their own senses of honor. My cheeks felt hot, but I didn't think my flushed skin showed in the dim light of the club. At least, I hoped it didn't.

I slipped my jacket back on, covering my tattoos. *Protective coloration,* I thought, imagining myself melting into invisibility in the gloom of the club, a tiny leaf-colored salamander keeping very still on a branch.

After a few cocktails, though, I rallied. The DJ was playing our table's requests back to back, and it was no longer possible to remain seated with all that booty-shaking music wooing me out onto the dance floor. I shoved my jacket under our table and went out to dance with my friends, male and female.

Stomping and whirling, my back slick with sweat and my tattoos transformed into brilliant plumage under the flashing lights, I felt murderously sensual. As I got on top and took the music between my thighs it fucked me back hard, pounding into my cunt and my belly, and my desire for myself at my freest and wildest rose up and set everything on fire, turning the walls of the club to gold and crimson.

As I danced, I saw the man who'd offered to buy me a drink and then insulted me. He was leaning into his beverage at a little table next to the bar, alone and gin-dazed. He'd taken my complicity in being his object of desire for granted, assuming that I'd dressed to attract him and others. Sensing my gaze, he glanced at me briefly then turned his attention back to his drink. His squalid, man-size desire was no match for mine, and we both knew it—what was a thousand times more important was what *I* wanted and how effortlessly I could take that desire and more from the friction between my hips.

Out on the dance floor with my beautiful, fierce friends, with the music moving inside me like a slow fist, I was burning hot—a feral thing, tearing through skin to meat with sharp teeth, stripping flesh from bone.

I may be a freaky bitch, but I'm a freaky bitch who can bust a serious move on the dance floor. And some nights that's all a freaky bitch needs.

THIS BOOK IS about fucking and food. The intersection of both sets is desire.

But desire itself is rarely uncomplicated. Desire can make us feel powerful, exultant, and free—but yearning can also be dangerous. Sometimes when we inspire desire, we're punished.

10

DESIRE

And sometimes when we allow others to lavish their desire on us, we end up needing a long, hot shower.

The chapters "Eating Out" and "Southbound" are two sides of the same you-are-what-you-eat coin. "Risk" finishes the set.

"Earl Grey Tea" is a love story. So is "Britney."

"Sploshing" delineates the perils of using food as erotic outerwear.

"Moules" is a DIY mash note to mollusks.

Don't be scared. Put this in your mouth, and swallow.

EATING OUT

A WARM TONGUE IN YOUR ASS IS LIKE BEING BABY-WIPED: an infantile exercise in gentle, soap-free cleaning, more about the idea of boundaryless porn star virtuosity than actual mind-blowing erotic sensation—or so I've found, anyway.

For a while there it seemed like all my male dates were pulling out oral-anal during our first sexual encounters, as if eating pussy proficiently suddenly wasn't enough to secure a return invitation to my boudoir. For three months, every man I took to bed chose to consider my hindquarters his own personal Old Country Buffet line, moving from carving station to (tossed) salad bar in predictable succession. It was as if they all subscribed to the same cheerfully salacious man-rag, a newsletter to which ladies were not privy: *This week, gentlemen—stun her with a hot, squirmy tongue in her back door!*

And I *was* stunned—the first time. Definitely the second time. But by the third time, and the fourth time, I began to wonder if they were all phoning each other and sharing helpful hints on a toll-free public information hotline about how to fuck me. And I really wanted to set the record straight with the man who was disseminating the idea that I wanted to impersonate a human salt lick in the bedroom. Because that man had his information wrong—dead wrong—but he sure was a vociferous son of a bitch. You had to admire his "British are coming!" enthusiasm. Too bad he wasn't circulating better intelligence. Because whenever I got my asshole licked, thanks to the misguided anal-evangelism of my own personal Paul Revere, it was *only* the British who were coming. I sure as hell wasn't. Being on the receiving end of an intestinal Wet Willy didn't get me hot. It just made me want to offer my lover du jour a mouthful of Listerine or a stick of sugar-free gum as I hastened him out my door, never to return.

True—after a career in adult modeling, my asshole was usually so clean you could eat off it, like my own personal hygienically pine-scented kitchen floor. I learned to relax—not to fight the baby wipe—not to tense up. I could do this by pretending to be a tiny kitten being cleaned all over by my mommy cat's raspy sand-tongue. Sometimes it even felt good, like using a washcloth in a steamy bath after a particularly laborious dump. But usually, my silent tolerance during the act stemmed from resignation: It was clear that I had some kind of ass-karma to live through, and that regardless of my preferences, it was best to let my lovers act on me as they wished. I learned to lie still, keeping my ass muscles helpfully loose. I tried to avoid any contemplation of vengeful farting.

And after a while, I found a man who *didn't* try to shove his tongue in my rectum on our first sexual romp, and after he made me come with his mouth on my pussy and his fingers inside me, I kissed him (on the mouth—you can do that when your lover's lips and tongue haven't just been up your rear) and declared myself done with mommy-cats and warm washcloths and human-tongue baby-wiping.

I have no regrets: My kitchen floor may be spotless, but I prefer serving dinner in an intimate location involving a little more ambience and romance.

SOUTHBOUND

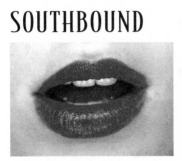

IT'S ORAL SEX IF YOU'RE FEELING CLINICAL, OR IF YOU'RE
trying to pretend you don't do it.

You might have decided that "going down" sounds too casual, "sucking dick" too self-consciously tough, "eating pussy" more information than necessary. You might be discussing an act you haven't done in ages, or an act that hasn't been performed on you in frustrating, maddening weeks by a lazy lover. So *oral sex* it is—a term so prim it's nearly virginal. *Oral sex? Why, no, thank you. I had a late lunch.*

But—it's *eating pussy* if you're sassy, talking tough, describing what makes you come or what you fantasize about doing to the hot girl at your gym. *Munching box* or *munching carpet* are retro terms for the same thing—but who has a "carpet" anymore in this age of hysterical depilation? Pubic rugs have gone the way of sanitary napkin belts, girdles, hot rollers, and pointed-cone bras. But naked or gloriously, anachronistically furry, *eating pussy* is all about the smooth slide into salt, a long slow dive into warmth and scent. There's no particular moment when you have to make a decision: swallow, or not? Girl-juice is a constantly fluctuating variable from start to finish. You go down, and from the moment you gently part labia and burrow in, you're drinking her like Scotch broth.

What about *sucking cock*—words that describe the man you love pushing his hips up and moaning with pleasure as you take him deep, because yes, you are that nasty, and yes, you want it that much, and yes, his whole world right now is his cock in your mouth, and you are breathless with the power and devotion of such intimate assembly.

And swallowing? I'll admit that when I think about all the come I've consumed in my life, the sheer volume becomes alarming. I imagine the restaurant-size jugs of mayonnaise occupying shelf space at Costco in a neat industrial phalanx. How many of those? And how many more, if I count the come that's splashed my tits, my ass, my face—and in one memorable instance, that shot up my nose in a reverse milk sneeze, dripping down my throat like cocaine for the next half hour? How many gallons—or, if you prefer, *liters*—in my whole life? The thought of that kind of quantity can really make a girl consider spitting instead.

But as much as I love *eating pussy* and *sucking cock*—and as many times as I've used both terms, rolling them around in my mouth deliberately like sips of fine, velvety Shiraz, really *tasting* them, sometimes to shock, sometimes for work, and sometimes, blessedly, with love—the part of each term that intrigues me isn't the direct object, it's the action words: *Eat* me. *Suck* me.

There's nothing clinical about those words at all.

And all of a sudden, consumption is back where it belongs—in the mouth, in the heart, in the cunt and the cock—living as need, experienced in physical desire as sharp as hunger or thirst. You wrap your mouth around something warm and salty and wet and suck on it like it's the only thing that will keep you alive. You taste the most intimate part of your lover. You gobble him or her up. You are a pig for him or her—your lover's juice runs down your chin and you want more. It's both simple and joyous, a communion during which your lover's body itself transubstantiates into your Bread of Life. Eat this and live forever.

When you eat someone—when you *go down, suck dick, lick pussy*—you consume them. You're taking them into your body and allowing their proteins, fats, and fluids to nourish you in an act intimate enough to be holy.

It is an act of love, make no mistake.

EARL GREY TEA

I WAS LONELY. I HADN'T HAD SEX SINCE I'D LEFT NEW YORK,
and that was six months earlier. Working as a stripper and a porn
star while being celibate was like bartending without ever actually getting to sit down and enjoy a cocktail. I wrote a personal ad
and sent it to *The Stranger* under Girls Seeking Girls.

> *Bad Girl Needs Spanking*
> *My heart belongs to Daddy.*

My ad had been out a week; I'd gotten a few calls. I was
surprised and dismayed at how many women seemed to be deliberately ignoring what I thought was obvious: I wasn't looking
for a wife, I was looking for someone to smack me around and

maybe fuck me. Also, I had used the term *Daddy* to indicate that I was looking for a butch, not someone androgynous or feminine. Perhaps I should have been clearer and written, *My heart belongs to Daddy*—not *to an annoying middle-management lipstick lezzy who shops at the Pottery Barn and lives in a condo on the Eastside who wouldn't know kinky sex if it shoved a strapped-on dick right up her flat, bony ass.*

I couldn't imagine being with a man after having worked as a lingerie model at Butterscotch's Live Lingerie Adult Tanning, a sleazy adult tanning operation, for half a year. Frankly, I was sick of men's shenanigans. No matter how attractive a man might look on the outside, it seemed like all you had to do was sit him down on a bath towel, walk into the room in your underwear, hand him some baby oil, and he'd turn into a greedy, leering pervert. Most of them just wanted to be watched while they shoved fingers or toys up their own butts, ate their own come, or tweaked their own nipples. It was as if they were *trying* to disgust us. The idea of dating one held no appeal.

And as much as I loved the way feminine girls looked, I didn't want hours of kissing and all the soft-focus faux-"lesbian" tit-rubbing they showed on the Playboy Channel to excite straight men. I get off by being fucked, hard—not by being kissed and patted. Dating another femme just seemed like we'd spend all our time fighting each other for the bathroom mirror, eating salads, and brushing each other's hair.

I wanted a butch. I wanted a strong, sexy, short-haired, cocksure butch lesbian who could lay me down on my back in the boudoir and make me feel like a woman. I wanted someone with a tool belt, a variety of toolish implements, and the know-how to get the job done right. I wanted someone who wanted to fuck me all nasty, the way I wanted to be fucked—who would know when to treat me like a slut and when to treat me like a little girl. I wanted Axl Rose crossed with Stanley Kowalski, with tits and a vagina. It was a tall order, but I had to trust that the clarity of my intention would generate the desired results. Also, what did I have to lose? It wasn't as if I were in danger of becoming any *less* fucked than I already was.

I hadn't bothered to call anyone back yet. Especially not the woman who specifically mentioned how much she loved the Pottery Barn in her voice mail message.

I HAD PRETTY much given up on my *Stranger* ad after two weeks. Every person who responded sounded wrong. They were either too feminine, or too dumb. One left me a joke and laughed—a *haw, haw, haw* that I cut off immediately by pressing DELETE. I couldn't imagine getting spanked by a woman who sounded like an extra on *Hee Haw*.

It was almost enough to turn a bisexual girl completely straight. I'd had boyfriends before. I considered checking Boys Seeking Girls to see if anyone seemed like a viable prospect. The main thing that stopped me—besides the thought of men sitting on towels and jerking their meat like unmedicated psychotics—was that a boy seeking a girl was more likely to have seen my porn, and to relate to me *as* a porn star. I didn't want to have sex with someone who just wanted to have sex with a girl they'd seen naked on the Internet. Besides, I read through all the Boys Seeking Girls ads and nobody sounded good. They all wanted relationships or no-strings-attached sex. I wanted something somewhere in between.

DESIRE

I also didn't want anyone who wanted me to be the decision-maker in the bedroom. At Butterscotch's, I *worked* as a dom! The last thing I wanted to do was work without pay for some cringing, demanding submissive. I thought it might be nice to get spanked for a change, instead of always being the one holding the paddle. Too many of the Boys Seeking Girls ads seemed like they could be written by customers.

I decided to check my *Stranger* voice mail one more time before deleting my account. It was just my luck: I could *sell* access to my vagina, but I couldn't give it away for free.

I called the number and punched in my code. I didn't go with 6969, though I'd been tempted to. I figured too many other ad-writing perverts would pick the same code. Instead I went with your classic 6666: the number of the Beast plus an extra six for *Extra Satanic Evil.*

I had one new call. A caller! A new one! Finally!

I pressed one for *play message.*

I heard a low chuckle.

"Well," the caller said. "Aren't you precious? I think you may be what I'm looking for. I'm Mick. I wouldn't mind spanking you, Princess. But you have to earn anything else."

Another low laugh. It sounded so *nasty.* Then she hung up.

Press four to replay your message. I pressed four. When it was done replaying, I pressed four again. I kept thinking I'd mis-heard. Was she really talking to me like this? *"Princess"?* I was breathless.

Press eight to return this call. I pressed it.

At the beep I said, "Hello, Mick? This is Sarah? You—" I cleared my throat. I forced myself to breathe. "You called my ad.

EARL GREY TEA

Would you like to meet me for, uh, tea? On Friday?" That was my next day off. I gave my phone number. My voice only shook a little.

Tea. I wondered if she liked tea. Her voice was so low and slow, it sounded like she drank a fifth of Scotch for breakfast, and chased the Scotch with a carton of unfiltered Marlboros.

I realized that I was wet between the legs.

Please call me back, Mick.

To distract myself I called the *Stranger* voice mail system again, punched in my code, and listened to her message five more times. Then I had to hurry up and bathe and shave to make it to my evening shift at work.

I felt wired, like I'd had too much coffee or cocaine.

I kept thinking of Mick's voice, and her unbearably sexy laugh.

THE NEXT DAY I got a message from Mick. She told me to meet her at Café Septième, on Broadway, for tea. At four. "Be prompt," she said. She sounded bemused.

Who the fuck was this Mick? *"Be prompt"?* I was beside myself. I didn't know if I liked being talked to like that or not.

I was used to customers and their insincere sycophancy. They attempted to stroke my ego in order to manipulate me, saying *You're so beautiful* but meaning *Touch my cock.* The dom clients pretended to respect me, but that was only because they fantasized about their own lack of power and subsumed will. Their wormy pseudo-deference was 100 percent about them—not about me at all. I could be a cardboard cutout in a corset propped up against the wall, and they'd abase themselves to the image of me just the same.

DESIRE

Mick didn't seem to give a shit either way, like I could show up or not—and if I did, maybe she'd check me out, and if I didn't, maybe she'd just drink Scotch and smoke a cigarette and stare off into the middle distance, while the ash on her cig got longer and longer and then finally dropped off.

It was maddening.

I BATHED, SHAVED, dressed, put on makeup. I was at Café Septième at 3:55 PM.

It was a chilly, white-skied afternoon. Gulls wheeled and shrieked, coming up to Capitol Hill from Elliott Bay, far from home. I wondered if they were looking for food or were just being adventurous. When they landed you could see the red spots on their beaks, the bull's-eyes where the little gulls tapped to take food from the mommy gull's mouth. The spots always looked like ketchup or blood to me.

I'd worn the wool coat I'd bought secondhand in New York. I hadn't had a chance to buy a new one yet. The sleeves were too short and my wrists were cold. I kept pulling them down, but the second I moved my arms they'd shrink back, leaving my wrists naked and vulnerable. I probably looked like a hick, or some overgrown freak of nature. *Was this bad karma for laughing at the* Hee Haw *woman?* I wondered.

I sat at the bar. Ordered tea. It was warm enough in the restaurant that I could take my coat off. I put it on the floor beneath my feet. There were cigarette butts on the floor, and it was visibly dirty. Maybe they were too cool to mop here.

The service at Septième was legendarily terrible, but

EARL GREY TEA

everyone who lived on Capitol Hill went there anyway. It was like you had to go because everyone else did. It was unavoidable. You could swear never to go there again, but eventually someone would say, "I'll meet you at Septième!" and you'd agree, and then suddenly, helplessly, you'd realize you'd just made plans to go back, even though you'd said you never would. You'd tell yourself, *Okay, but this is the last time I'm going there*, but you knew you'd be back. It was like the Bermuda Triangle of restaurants: It pulled you in, again and again.

You could always tell the people who didn't live on the Hill because they'd order the stale desserts that sat out on the table near the front door. Those desserts were always there—they never seemed to get wrapped up or put away. They were dry and sometimes moldy.

"Would you like a slice of cake to go with your tea?" asked my waiter. He was tiny, with one pierced ear.

"No thank you," I said. *I'm no tourist, jerk.*

AT FOUR, EXACTLY, Mick arrived.

She took off a cracked leather coat and put it on the stool next to her. Underneath she wore a series of men's shirts, layered one over the other. She smelled like cigarettes. I inhaled her scent like a child.

Mick was handsome, but mostly she was *sexy*, lit up from the inside. She glowed like a candle. It was like she made her own light. It moved with her. How could someone be as bright as that, throw off so much energy? It almost crackled around her, like an electric field.

DESIRE

She took off her battered hat and shook out her hair. It was bleached blond, sleek and soldierly, shaved on the sides and falling in lank chunks over her forehead. My own mane was long and had a horrible tendency to curl.

Her complexion was olive, and her cheekbones were high. *All* her bones were apparent. I'd never liked skinny girls before, but Mick made it seem right. Her pants hung off her hip bones, her shoulders were angular—it was like she didn't *need* flesh to be sexy. Her bones were her frame, and everything else was flayed away as needless.

Compared to Mick I was too tall, too fat, too fleshy. She was stripped down like a muscle car, compact—nothing but movement and speed and elegant lines. Beside her I felt horribly plush and decadent—all tits and ass. All *flesh.* She seemed like she didn't need anything in this world to survive, except for black coffee and maybe the occasional bump of crystal meth or cocaine. In contrast, I *wanted.* I ate, I shat, I craved. Her distance from the corporeal world was alien to me.

I was ashamed of myself. I felt giant and lumbering next to her.

There were deep blue circles under Mick's eyes, but when she smiled at me, her eyes sparkled. She seemed so alive.

My face felt hot.

"Hi," she said. "I'm Mick."

Like honey over broken glass, I thought.

"Funny, you don't look Irish," I said. I had to force myself not to say anything else, not to giggle.

Remember to keep your mouth shut. You can't go wrong if you don't say anything.

"Like Mick Jagger," she said. She laughed.

"I know," I said.

Mick ordered her own pot of tea from the tiny waiter. Earl Grey.

Her tea choice seemed sophisticated to me, like what you'd ask for if you were European and sitting in a sidewalk café somewhere in the Montmartre. I had tried to like Earl Grey in the past, but to me it always just tasted like hot perfume or like dry wine: tannic, with an herbal aftertaste. I liked to drink sweet things, not things that seemed like they sucked all the moisture out of my mouth while I drank them. Astringent wine and bitter tea just seemed like unnecessary punishment.

I preferred English breakfast with real cream and real sugar. I never drank to the bottom of my cup because I didn't like the wet tea-leaf fragments in the last few sips. Supposedly some fortune tellers could read those tea leaves and predict what was going to happen to you. I wondered if the leaves actually spelled out words, or if they formed pictures, or if the deal was more like *how many* leaves and where they stuck to the sides of the cup.

Mick drank her Earl Grey plain and hot. The scent of the lavender oil mixing with Mick's smells made me feel drunk. I wanted to lean forward and press my face against her chest and just breathe in her scents forever.

I noticed our waiter hadn't asked Mick if she wanted cake.

"So, Mick," I said. "What do you do for a living?" I hated asking that question. It made it sound like I was interviewing her for a job—though in a way, I was. Honestly, I just wondered what a creature like herself could possibly do in the mundane world. I couldn't see her in a cubicle. Her radiance would distract everyone, beaming up from behind the walls of her partitioned space like a spotlight. Besides, what would she wear? A suit? A skirt? Some sort of Gertrude Stein–ish ensemble?

"I'm a rock star," she said, slowly and sardonically. The way she drew the words out it was like *rock star* was in quotes—as if she were making fun of the whole rock star thing, or the whole fantasy of being a rock star, or of my question, or of me for asking something so standard and small.

Was she a rock star? Was she just teasing me? Was she waiting for me to go *Wow!* and start asking questions like *Which band are you in?* so she could laugh at my gullibility? I felt like a dumb kid asking for an autograph, unsure of how to interact with someone who so exceeded my own social ease.

"What's your *career trajectory*, pretty girl?" The invisible quotation marks again.

"I'm a stripper. I also model," I said. I didn't feel like I needed to go into the fact that my modeling mostly consisted of plugging up my various orifices with plastic toys, and that my pictorials were mostly on the Internet instead of in glossy magazines.

"A stripper," Mick said, contemplatively. "Well, that's cool. You like it?"

"It's fine," I said. "The money's decent."

We drank our tea.

"You want to take a walk?" said Mick.

We put on our coats. I felt ashamed of my wool coat with the too-short sleeves. Mick's leather coat looked as if she'd been born in it, or born to wear it. It smelled like a million different last calls at a million different bars. It smelled like various interchangeable intrigues with scores of beautiful, tragic women, and Mick saying,

EARL GREY TEA

"Baby, I love you, but I got to go." I knew that what I was picturing was corny and probably not even true, but it was still affecting.

It was the kind of affecting that made my panties wet. I had worn my black see-through boy-cut ones with lace, just in case.

I was taller than Mick. But then again, I was wearing big chunky-heeled platform shoes, so I was taller than everyone. My height didn't mean anything—it was a cheat, like an underwire bra or the clear mascara I used to keep my eyebrows neatly groomed. I figured that flat-footed we'd probably be eye to eye. The thought of being that close to Mick thrilled me.

We walked down Broadway toward Seattle Central Community College, then we crossed the street and walked back. The air smelled so good—tidal, like salt water. I loved winter, and I was glad it was coming.

I took Mick's arm. She moved my hand from the bend of her elbow and held it instead.

We were holding hands. Everyone could see that we were a couple. We *weren't* a couple really, of course, but I felt like everyone who passed us was looking at us and smiling and going, *Oh, how adorable: lesbians!* Lesbians were way cuter than gay men. Two gay men holding hands just looked like some kind of political statement. Lesbian hand-holding was softer, and sweeter.

I had never understood the word *lighthearted* before. I'd never thought of it as an actual, physical description, like a symptom you'd describe to a doctor. I'd thought *lighthearted* was more metaphoric, something that had meaning only to poets or other insufferably sensitive individuals, like the kind of old ladies who gardened and said stuff like *happy as a lark*. But my heart really *did* feel light, like it was up near my throat and weightless. I felt like I'd taken a hit of acid—the lifting sensation I was experiencing, walking down the street with Mick, was weirdly similar to the first rush of a lush, sensual trip coming on. It was like free-fall, if falling didn't scare you. Or like falling *up* into the silvery winter sky.

"I was just thinking," she remarked, "about how much I love Seattle when it's cold. I love the rain and the short days. Do you?" There were no invisible quotation marks in her words. She sounded thoughtful, and a little sad.

"I feel the same way," I said.

"Do you want to come home with me?" Again, her voice was grave.

"Yes," I said. I did. I wanted to very badly. I wanted privacy with Mick, to see if she'd try to kiss me, if she even *wanted* to. But I was also deeply curious about where she lived. It was like I wanted to know everything I could about her all at once. I was gobbling up information. Again, it was that acidy feeling of suddenly having a dozen senses, instead of only five. I felt keenly open, and aware, and awake.

We walked up John Street, toward Fifteenth Avenue, to her apartment. Her building was a big white run-down house with a sagging porch facing a sad, muddy little front yard. There were a bunch of battered bikes chained with actual chains and padlocks to the porch and the front steps, the way the squatter kids on Broadway locked up their bikes. Some bikes were missing wheels.

The front door was unlocked, and Mick pushed it open. The hall inside was very dark and had that apartmenty smell of roach spray, gas ovens, old food, and ancient, ghostly cigarettes. There were posters thumbtacked to the walls alongside flyers for bands and lost pets. The walls had been spackled, but nobody had pained

EARL GREY TEA

over the white spots, so the spackle stood out like scabs. There was a pile of *Stranger*s under the mailboxes. I wondered if that was where Mick got her copy of the issue that featured my ad.

I felt immediately comfortable. It was a dive, a punk rock hippie house. I bet the tenants stayed up late and played their stereos loud, and I bet nobody ever knocked on the walls or complained, because they were up late playing their music, too. In houses like this, *roommate* was a nebulous concept, made up of whoever was crashing with you for days or weeks and chipping in with rent money, drugs, or groceries. Sometimes you had roommates, and sometimes you didn't. It depended on who was in town, who you were dating, and which of your friends had gotten kicked out, fired, or evicted.

The turned-up thump of someone's bass from upstairs made me feel safe and at home. The bass line was jumpy and crazy. Was it Primus? I loved apartment buildings where in the middle of a working day people were home, smoking weed and cranking up their music.

I figured people probably ate a lot of Top Ramen here.

We walked down the hall. I smelled cat pee and, sure enough, the sweet, insidious odor of pot.

Mick reached her door. We paused while she pulled keys on a long chain out of her pants pocket. The top half of the door was mostly covered by a big poster for the band Hater. I made a mental note to check out Hater at the used-CD store on lower Broadway. Mick was the coolest person I'd ever met, and I figured Hater would probably be really good. Plus, if she said anything about them, I could sound knowledgeable. Maybe I could even bring them up casually sometime when we weren't at the apartment, so it wouldn't look like I was just bringing them up because of the poster.

DESIRE

Her apartment was one huge room, with a futon against one wall. There were clothes everywhere. Her scent pushed into my face as we entered. Concentrated eau de Mick. There were posters on every wall, so many that some of them were layered over each other. I noticed a big one of David Bowie—the red one with his face in black-and-white makeup from *Diamond Dogs*.

I was never a huge Bowie fan, frankly. But now I wanted to be. I wanted to like the same things Mick liked. Bowie was okay, it was just that so many of his songs seemed dreary and overly orchestrated.

I preferred faster, heavier music. I liked Alice in Chains a lot—the way Layne Staley's voice soared over the slamming, sludgy bass, and the way Jerry Cantrell harmonized with him. Sometimes when I listened to Alice in Chains, I imagined that Layne Staley was in love with me and was writing songs about me. I also thought about him fucking me, spreading my legs and holding me down. I didn't know if he was handsome, but I figured anyone who could sing the way he could was probably dirty and sexy enough to leave his boots and Levi's on while he fucked me.

Sometimes, I imagined, he left his cowboy hat on, too.

There were dried flowers, furniture, books, and records everywhere. I couldn't look around enough—there was so much to take in.

"Please, sit down," Mick said. I sat on the bed. The futon mattress was bare. There were a few blankets crumpled down on one end plus bunches of clothes all matted and tangled around each other. It looked like a nest, not a bed.

From the way the blankets were kicked down to the foot of the mattress, I guessed Mick probably didn't sleep much—or

31

didn't sleep well. That would explain the dark circles under her eyes. I wondered if she had insomnia, or nightmares, or if she was just too crackling with energy to actually lie down and sleep.

Though it was only late afternoon, the light was already fading. Mick fussed with the stereo and put on something I didn't recognize. It was surprisingly pretty—I wouldn't have guessed she'd have picked something so girlish. I didn't mind that she hadn't bothered to turn on the overhead light—the room was dim, but not dark. I thought, *In half an hour the sun will be down and one of us will turn on the lights, and all of a sudden it will be bright and cozy inside and cold and dark outside, and maybe I'll just stay.*

Mick sat next to me. I put my head on her shoulder.

We sat, listening to the music.

After a little while Mick kissed me. Her lips were so soft. Her tongue tasted of lavender and felt as soft as old velvet.

As the light disappeared, we lay together on a bed of discarded clothes. Neither of us got up to turn on the lights.

The music ended, and for hours all I heard through the speakers was the record player's needle, softly and endlessly bumping against the last groove of the last track.

THREE DAYS LATER, in a sweet haze, I left her apartment to buy food for us. In the tea and coffee aisle of the grocery store, I spied a tiny metal box of loose Earl Grey tea. Slipping off the lid of the box, I inhaled deeply.

And sure enough, under the bergamot and the dusty smell of the tea itself, twining around and through the smell of lavender like a long, sweet kiss, was the scent of Mick's creaky leather jacket.

32

DESIRE

SPLOSHING

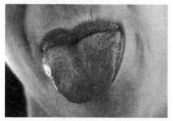

"SPLOSHING" IS A SPECIFIC FETISH INVOLVING NAKED GIRLS
and messy food. I've seen pictures on the Internet of everything
from a series of bare asses planted firmly in birthday cakes to a
good-humored nude model languishing in a bathtub filled with
baked beans. Even Annie Leibovitz wasn't above photograph-
ing Whoopi Goldberg in a tub of milk. Whoopi's skin glowed
like chocolate and her broad smile was telling: She was having
fun romping naked in milk.

I have to admit that sploshing isn't a fetish I find personally compelling—generally, I prefer food *in* me to food *on* me. And
despite the undeniable down-home charm of using fruits and vegetables in lieu of manufactured sex toys, I've never met an ear of
corn I've liked enough to take to bed. When it comes to produce,
I just want to be friends.

An ex-girlfriend taught me to mix olive oil with hair conditioner, half and half. You apply the resulting masque to your hair, put a plastic grocery bag over your slimy locks to catch any drips, and—if you're really on a mission—use a hairdryer over the bag to heat the conditioner mayonnaise inside, which allows the moisture to penetrate even more efficiently. After an hour or so, remove the bag and rinse. Your hair will be astoundingly soft. Your scalp may smell a tiny bit salady, but if you keep the ratio one to one, the conditioner fragrance should cover up most of the olive oil smell. Because I regularly bleach my hair to powder, pan-frying my scalp in the process, I use this deep-conditioning treatment a few times a month. So far, my hair is still attached to my head and doesn't entirely resemble fiberglass, so I count that as a success.

You can mash up avocados and apply them to your skin as a moisturizing masque, or so I've heard. If you want to be really fancy, you can add honey to the mashed-up avocados. Or you can make an exfoliating scrub of honey, oatmeal, and plain whole-milk yogurt.

But these are all things I'd rather eat, given the choice.

A FRIEND OF mine who grew up in Southern California told me a story about the dog her family had when she was a little girl. One summer, the dog inexplicably grew a long, lush coat of glossy hair—nobody knew why, but all of a sudden its fur was soft and thick and *fragrant* instead of coarse and doggy. My friend spent hours brushing the dog's shiny coat, marveling at its shampoo commercial-caliber body and bounce. Everyone commented on the thickness and softness of the dog's hair, from neighbors to strangers on the street. Everyone wanted to know what brand of kibble the dog was being fed.

One day my friend followed the family dog into the back yard, wanting to brush and pet it. All of a sudden the reason for the dog's glossy mane became evident: It had been gorging on the avocados that had fallen into their yard from the neighbors' tree. Once avocado season was over, the dog's coat returned to normal. My friend still brushed the dog every now and again out of a sense of duty, but the sensual enjoyment she'd taken in the dog's wonderfully conditioned fur was gone. The Breck dog was no more.

I'VE HAD A lot of experience with food-sex. I've been dribbled with honey, sprayed with canned whipped cream, and topped with hot fudge. I've been fed a variety of foods from other people's fingers. I've given blow jobs with Altoids tucked into my cheeks like a minty-fresh squirrel, and I've sucked on ice cubes and then nipples more times than I can count.

But all in all, I find erotic eating upsetting—maybe I'm just not enough of a multitasker, but I prefer not to mix the process of digestion and excretion with anything romantic. I'd rather enjoy a slice of birthday cake on a plate than scraped from the ass of an attractive acquaintance—and a tub full of baked beans just seems like a plumbing disaster (and a vicious yeast infection) waiting to happen. I admit to being old and no fun in matters where food is used as a prop for sex.

If I'm cramming fresh strawberries into my mouth, cramming them into my coochie just seems redundant. And if I'm going down on a girl, I want to taste her, not an array of dessert toppings. The Altoid trick is just weird and robotic. And drizzling chocolate sauce anywhere near someone's asshole just seems blatantly scatological.

Isn't good food sexy enough on its own?

A FEW YEARS ago I became aware of a phenomenon occurring in a few publicity-hungry Japanese restaurants. Apparently, for a steep price, the restaurant will hire a model to lie naked and still on a table. The model's body is then covered in sushi—sometimes leaves modestly conceal private areas—and then restaurant guests are allowed to pluck mouthfuls of sushi from the motionless body with their chopsticks. It is all presented in a very jolly way.

First of all, I'd prefer that my sushi not sit at body temperature for too long. Raw fish, body heat, and the ambient bacteria that live on human skin seem like a bad, bad combination. And— no offense to any of the models—but I don't even share Chapstick with my friends. I can't see myself eating a tuna roll from someone's pubes, leaf-covered or not.

And, having spent a career being a malleable, living body for pay, I can't help but identify with the sushi models. How trying would it be to lie absolutely still for several hours as sake-laced businessmen and their expense-account guests poked at you with wooden sticks? You can't tell me your skin wouldn't crawl. You can't tell me you wouldn't stare up into their faces and wonder what would motivate someone to pay a large amount of money for the novelty of using a human body as a piece of furniture—a warm, living table—nothing more. You can't tell me you wouldn't get chilly as you lay there waiting for them to finish. You can't tell me you wouldn't have to pee. You can't tell me you wouldn't flinch when some red-faced clown used his chopsticks to pinch your nipple, pretending to mistake your flesh for a rosette of pickled ginger or a bit of smoked salmon.

Something seems deeply pornographic about eating sushi from a living model, and it's not the paid nudity.

Treating a fellow human being as an inert, insensate object is a depraved act, whether you're jerking off to pictures of them on the Internet or eating food taken from the surfaces of their bodies. Whether they're getting paid to pretend to be a school-girl or a serving tray, pleasure necessitates them being viewed as something other than an actual living, breathing, thinking, feeling individual.

And maybe the models don't give two shits about what the people eating nigiri from their skin think about them. They probably don't. But that's not the point—I've been a paid model, and while nobody's ever eaten sashimi off of me, I've never felt victimized by my decision to pose for sexually explicit fare. I've cashed my paychecks and paid my bills without a sliver of curiosity about who would be spanking it to my images later. I couldn't have cared less if some greasy pervert mistook me for a Catholic schoolgirl *or* a piece of furniture, as long as I was making a fair wage for my work.

I'm not worried about the feelings of the models as much as I'm worried about the feelings of the restaurant patrons. I'm worried about the heads and hearts of folks who can do what they do. I think it's really bad for us to get used to viewing other people as *things*. I think it really hurts us. As much as we like to believe we can tell the difference between a living model and a table, there seems to be a great deal of confusion between porn models and living, feeling women. Either way—tables or bodies—they are objects for us to use without any consideration for their comfort or sensibilities.

I find this willingness to suspend belief in other people's basic humanity very, very dangerous.

I LIKE SUSHI a lot, and I love naked women. But I have no desire to go to one of those sushi restaurants that hire living models as serving platters. I also have no desire to look at a naked woman's body unless we're both in the same room together and she's naked because she wants to be—not because she's trying to pay her rent.

As the Offspring say, you gotta keep 'em separated.

DESIRE

RISK

I'M A RISK-TAKER. I'VE ALWAYS TAKEN RISKS—WITH MY body *and* my heart, with my mind and my emotions and my health. I'm a gambler, baby. I'd rather play steep odds for the big payoff than live my life wishing I'd had the courage to stake it all and win.

Furthermore, I'm at peace with losing. I've gotten my heart broken more times than I can count, and I'm carrying an extra twenty pounds of ballast on my ass and thighs from all the food I've gobbled up just because it tasted so good I didn't want to stop. When it comes down to the choice between living a life of *yes, please* and living one of *no, thanks* I'll choose *yes* every time, and I'll generally raise you a *can I have some more?* just to keep the stakes high.

I'm risking my health when I eat certain foods that I love, gambling that I'll be able to consume them without suddenly clutching my chest and falling over dead on the floor. I'm gambling with long-term systemic stuff like colon cancer, diabetes, and obesity, too, just in case the idea of keeling over with a heart attack before I reach the age of forty isn't serious enough. I know this. I'm not stupid. I read enough scary health news to know that when you snack on a pound of chocolate-covered bacon, you're holding your own life in your cupped, greasy hands. One fumble and your candy-covered-pork-eating days are over. There are a plethora of ways to ruin your own health, and many of them are quite delicious. Despite the risk, I eat—and love—with passionate enthusiasm. I've never been good at turning down the offer of something sweet.

WHEN I CAME of age (which is a polite way of saying *When I started to fuck*) in the mid-'80s, AIDS was the cause du jour, the hip concern that inspired legions of socially conscious, breathlessly virginal high schoolers to distribute condoms to their classmates, spreading the gospel of Safe Sex to people who probably wouldn't be having sex—safe or otherwise—until college.

Condoms came in all colors and flavors. Their packaging was fun and bright and sassy, incorporating cartoon characters and good-natured puns. The Stealth Condom ("They'll never see you coming!") was a popular and much-coveted item. Girls in training bras earnestly debated the merits of vanilla versus strawberry flavoring on condoms meant for safe fellatio, pressing their tongues to the unwrapped condoms as if licking stamps for their scrapbooks.

Condoms used to be mysterious and dirty—accoutrements for the Dirty Old Man set, not fresh, young, middle-class teens—but in the mid-'80s all that changed, and decidedly so: Millions of Junior Anti-Sex League honor students handily demonstrated prophylactic use with bananas years before any of them would ever encounter a hard and urgent phallus. Condoms became first chic accessories, then necessary social items.

I had a stash myself—Beyond 7s, Rough Riders, Trojan Magnums, and Trojan-Enz Larges functioned both as punch lines in their own right among the jock-and-stoner set *and* as jerkoff material in my solitary hours, years before I'd even experienced my first chaste kiss. Through osmosis, I learned that lubricated was better than nonlubricated and that the ones with nonoxynol-9 were the best of all, though they tasted soapy. I preferred vanilla flavoring to strawberry.

As we grew up and started to fuck, most of us paid lip service to our years of Safe Sex indoctrination: We used condoms. We used them proficiently, squeezing the latex receptacle tip and neatly rolling them down all the way, making sure to add water-based lubricant, and holding on to them firmly before dismounting. We fucked like middle-aged Bunny Ranch hookers, pragmatic and shameless as we garbed ourselves (and our lovers) in latex. It was like taking a vitamin or going to the gym: We were self-righteously Doing The Right Thing, Protecting Ourselves.

Decades later we would realize the risks of contracting AIDS from each other had been almost nil. We could have been fucking ourselves raw in a great big pileup without worrying about anything more distressing than breaking out before a school dance. Imagining ourselves as jaded libertines in need of protection was exciting but, sadly, almost completely inaccurate—most of us were virgins, and the rest of us were woefully inexperienced. In retrospect, our panic over disease transmission seemed a lot like wishful thinking.

Once I actually started using condoms for intercourse in my junior year of high school, I quickly became disenchanted. It turned out that condoms were far better in theory than in practice. Condoms were messy, inconvenient, and smelly! The studs and ribs didn't do a thing to increase "her" pleasure! The flavors made them taste *worse*, not better! And dental dams were just insane—how could a tiny square of latex cover an entire vulva? And more importantly, why would you want to lick bubble-gum-scented rubber when the whole point of cunnilingus was close, hot, tongue-to-cunt contact?

Plus, I was on the Pill. If I wasn't going to get pregnant—and if I was serially monogamous with men and women I loved and trusted—and if I got tested for HIV regularly—why, I thought, should I have to use condoms and all the other assorted hateful accessories? I didn't see the point, since two uninfected lovers couldn't infect each other! In the '90s, though, the idea of fucking without latex was suicidal heresy, so I kept my doubts to myself.

But cautiously, slowly, furtively, I began having unprotected sex.

It was my secret—like being bulimic or alcoholic. I didn't tell my friends. I continued to publicly debate the relative merits of Japanese- versus American-made condoms, between "thin" condoms and the ones sold—confusingly—as "extra-strength." I owned three different kinds of dental dams—mint, bubble-gum, and unscented. I kept a box of latex gloves under my bed. My boudoir smelled like a Goodyear tire. I kept up appearances.

DESIRE

At first I wasn't assertive about my preference for bareback lovin', and I'd allow a partner to put on a condom or slide on a glove, if he or she wanted to. But eventually I became active in my safe-sex discouragement, purring "I want to feel you inside me" in a way calculated to be irresistible. And I did want that—I wanted it very much. I wanted closeness, intimacy, and connection during sex. I wanted the boundaries between my body and my lovers' bodies to blend and melt. It was only right that an act so emotionally charged carried risk—I wanted to be vulnerable. The risk of death gave sex acknowledgeable weight, made it a sacred act. It was the opposite of casual—for me, sex was crucial. The hardware got in the way, lowered the stakes, turned intercourse into slapstick. I couldn't stand to reduce sex to a series of precautionary acts when, to me, it felt like something holy.

"I'm clean," I'd say to a potential sexual partner. "Are you?" I'd look in their eyes. I didn't fuck the ones I didn't trust to give me a true answer. I let myself be vulnerable to the ones I trusted, allowing them to take my life in their hands.

And I *was* clean—I got tested every six months, like clockwork. It was Lotto-rare when a chosen partner balked any further, despite all our social conditioning. I gleefully continued to evade condom use privately while publicly espousing only the safest of possible sex acts. I was Dr. Jekyll and Mr. Hyde: virtuous and upright in the company of other safe-sex aficionados, and dangerously depraved in secret.

I learned to orgasm, clenching my muscles and then releasing them with a *whoosh!* when I felt a male partner coming inside me. Afterward, I'd feel satisfied, primal. It was a feeling I did not get when denied my partner's sexual fluids. Likewise, a woman's bare hand in my cunt was different than a latexed one: A bare hand could reach up inside me all the way to my heart. I learned to let myself open up, to feel afraid, to take the leap, to trust.

The condoms and dental dams and gloves in my bedroom grew brittle and dusty, taking up the valuable space I preferred to fill with water-based lubricant, toys, and packets of Ortho-Novum 7/7/7. Eventually, I threw all my latex fashion accessories away. I was an outlaw in the company of other outlaws. And that felt pretty good.

I've never had any STDs. Not even a single cold sore. I've never been pregnant, either. The only thing I have to show for my years of promiscuity is a broken hymen and a slightly battered heart, two old friends living together in close proximity.

Of course, after twenty years of having sex with a slew of different partners and for a variety of different reasons—some of them good, and some of them pretty piss-poor, if you want to know the truth—there are a few fucks I wish I could take back. And the more I think of fucks I wish I could take back, the more names and faces pop up in my brain. It's daunting, all right.

But who am I trying to kid? My whole life has been an "experimental" phase, both sexually and culinarily speaking. I've put some fucked-up shit in my mouth, for sure. It's just that I'm less afraid of getting my heart broken or suffering the consequences of a bad erotic choice than I am of not taking every chance I can on love, deliciousness, honesty, and Vulcan mind-melding sex. I don't want to live in fear. I want to live boldly and with as much love and desire as the world sees fit to offer me.

I've had my slutty phases, but I'm pretty conservative these days, if you want to know the truth.

44

DESIRE

I'm monogamous, devoutly in love with a man I fucked on the first date with no condom, because I trusted him when he said he'd been tested a few months ago, and because I wasn't lying when I said I had too.

I fucked him without a condom because I wanted to feel him inside me without any boundaries or reserve. Because his hands on me were right. Because his tongue in my mouth was heaven. Because the taste of his sweat burned me to ashes, from which I rose again—brand new, pure, and changed. Since then, every time we fuck my love is transformed, evolving into something deeper in the crucible of my little bed.

And yes, it is unsafe.

Yes, an act that sacred, that pleasurable, might hurt you. If done wrong, or with the wrong person, that act can kill. One mistake and you're dead, *bang bang*—if there's anything I learned from all the pretty girls solemnly handing out condoms in ninth grade homeroom, it's that. One ill-considered fuck equals you're dead. *Treat every person as if they're infected. AIDS kills.* I really was paying attention. And I don't take any of that lightly, nor do I have anything but respect for people who choose to use condoms, gloves, plastic wrap, and dams when they fuck. People living with HIV (or other systemic diseases like hepatitis C or herpes) don't have the luxury of the kind of choices I get to make, and I am deeply conscious of my privilege. I've been lucky—really lucky—while other people have gambled everything and suffered annihilating loss.

But I've always believed that true delight is worth some risk, whether it's a wild gustatory fracas of fried meat and fat and salt, or whether it's an act looked down upon by people who prefer to

45

ignore the holy communion that occurs when two people share their bodies with each other in every aspect.

It's a continual balancing act, weighing joy against fear. Do we play it safe and take the sure bet, living carefully and treating our bodies like fragile, easily broken glass, or sometimes—maybe only once in a great while—do we throw caution and good sense to the wind and revel in the taste of flesh between our teeth?

I have eaten well in my life, and I have loved well, and I will joyfully do every bit of it again, over and over, until I am wholly consumed—burned to ash by sheer bliss.

DESIRE

MOULES MARINIÈRE

MUSSELS ARE GOOD BECAUSE THEY'RE SUPEREASY TO MAKE
and fun to eat, and it's kind of romantic and messy and garlicky
to share a bowl and sop up the mussel broth with big torn shards
of bread. You must drink lots and lots of wine, and for dessert
it's very nice to have a small amount of high-quality chocolate[1] to
share afterward.

Here's what you do for the mussels:

Go to your fishmonger. If you're a hot girl, dress cute
and prepare to flirt. I don't care if you're gay—access to prime

---

1. Keep your chocolate at room temperature, otherwise the texture will be all off.
If you're going to eat cold chocolate, you may as well be eating a block of brown
wax. In the summer you can store your chocolate in the refrigerator, but pull it
out before you start cooking the main meal and it will be buttery and melty and
ready to eat by dessert time.

seafood trumps sexual preference any day. You are creating a relationship with someone who is very, very important. Know his name, greet him, ask him what's good. Make friends with him! Your fishmonger will make the difference between *meh* fish and *holy shit, that's good!* fish.

Ask him for a couple pounds of fresh, live mussels. Flirt now! Flirt flirt flirt! Because you have to ask him to go through his mussels, and to only give you the ones that are vibrantly alive. You're asking him to individually sort them for your princessy ass, and that's a big favor. So be sweet about it. If you are ingratiating enough, you will be rewarded with a few pounds of mussels that are healthy and ready to be cooked. If you're a dick about it, he'll just throw them into your package, and you'll have a bunch of dead mussels that are only good to be thrown out. Be nice! If he's busy, come back. Because he's well within his rights to just give you however many pounds of mussels you ask for, dead and alive.

Once you have your two pounds of fresh, live mussels, take them home and put them into a big mixing bowl. Fill the bowl with an inch or two of water, then wet a cloth towel and put that over the bowl. Refrigerate the bowl with the cloth over it—this will keep the mussels comfortable and alive until you're ready to cook them.

Okay, so fast-forward to when you're ready to make your mussels. It's best if you have a hot boy or girl to cook for, because they're gonna be all impressed with you and will want to fuck you afterward (especially if you tell them to bring wine and then have them sit and talk and drink with you while you cook).

Now it's time to sort the mussels. Put the bowl of refrigerated mussels in your sink and run cold water next to the bowl.

Now take out a mussel and look at it. It should be closed tight, or just barely open a sliver. Ones that are open are dead. Throw them out. Also throw out any mussels with cracked shells, or if the mussel part is protruding out of the shell, or if anything just seems weird or wrong or gives you a bad vibe. Wash the healthy ones under the cold water really, really well. You can use a little brush, but I normally just use my fingertips to get all the sand off. It's okay if the cold water makes them open or close a bit—they're living creatures, responsive to temperature change. This is good.

You will notice on the side of the mussel a little tuft of what looks like seaweed or, um . . . what else does it look like? Well, actually, kind of like *pubes*. I know this is gross—hang on, though. Rip off the wiry hairs (they should come off easily, in one tangled clump). This is called *bearding* the mussels. This sounds weird and gross but it's totally not. You're simply removing their little beards because you don't want to be eating that. I keep a paring knife handy for stubborn beard strands that just won't tear off.

Put all your washed, bearded mussels into a clean mixing bowl. Cover them with the damp towel and pop them back in the fridge.

Now: The hard part is done. Dinner's going to come together really fast at this point, so give your guest a loaf of good bread (I like sourdough, but a good rosemary bread is nice too) and a cutting board and have him or her slice the loaf into thick crusty pieces. Drink more wine.

Into a stockpot or very large, high-sided skillet, place three or four small, chopped shallots. (*Not* onions—onions aren't right. It really does need to be shallots.)

Chop up a bunch of fresh garlic and toss that in too. Throw

in half a stick of butter (not margarine, *never ever ever*, no matter what). If you're feeling fancy, you can cook some strips of bacon ahead of time and use the bacon fat instead of butter, crumbling the cooked bacon in with the shallots and garlic, but whatevs.

Heat the shallots, garlic, and butter over medium heat. Put the lid on. You are sweating the shallots, not sauteeing them. That basically means you're cooking them to translucency but not browning them. Shake the pot around a bit while you're sweating the shallots, so they don't stick and so the butter distributes.

Throw in herbs: dill, thyme, rosemary, freshly ground black pepper. Use bunches and bunches of each.

Once your shallots are almost-clear and soft, pour in *either* a few glasses of white wine *or* a few bottles of some kind of lager. (Like Foster's—a lightish beer. Don't use a dark one like Guinness. Budweiser and other American canned beers are actually fine for this.) Heat until the liquid is simmering. Then simmer awhile, leaving the lid off so the steam can escape. You're cooking the beer or wine down and allowing the alcohol to evaporate, leaving only the condensed flavor of the liquid. Have more wine. At this point your kitchen should be smelling incredibly good.

Now take the mussels out of the fridge and dump them into the simmering liquid. The liquid won't cover the mussels—it should only be a few inches in the bottom of the pot. Cover the pot with the lid, and leave it alone for five minutes.

After five minutes pull the pot off the heat. With the lid still on, shake the pot around. Peek in. Make sure the mussels have opened. If a bunch of them haven't, put the lid on and put the pot back on the heat for a minute more. Literally *a* minute.

Mussels cook fast, and you don't want to overcook them. The ones that still don't open are dead, and no amount of cooking will make them open.

Now pour the mussels and broth into a big bowl. Get a smaller bowl for the discarded shells. Put plenty of napkins on the table and a fork for each of you.

Now eat the fuck out of those amazing, delicious mussels, you fine-ass cook, you. Lick your fingers and sop up the broth with lots and lots of bread. Your whole house will smell like garlic and herbs and good, fresh shellfish, and your neighbors will fucking die and wish to God they were over at your place eating whatever it is you just made.

Afterward, drink more wine and eat some room-temperature chocolate.

Fall asleep full of good food. You may be too full to fuck, but amazingly enough, this will be totally okay. Sometimes your food fucks you so well that getting touched by another person is completely, blissfully beside the point.

BRITNEY

I LOVE BRITNEY SPEARS, AND I'M NOT ASHAMED OF IT.

Do I own any of her CDs? No, I do not. I have "Toxic" on my iPod because I used to perform to that song in the filthy, semilegal titty bars of New Orleans. It amused me to play such a sprightly all-American booty-shaker as an accompaniment to the desultory fucking motions I made slumped against the pole (or, if the dollar bills were flowing, on all fours). I relished performing as the Anti-Britney, with my chunky legs and my heavy metal tattoos: Dancing to "Toxic" both mocked and multiplied the dismal squalor of my surroundings. I loved inflicting it on my customers the way a particularly cruel prison warden might enjoy forcing his inmates to sing carols on Christmas Eve.

But aside from "Toxic," I don't care for Britney's music much.

I couldn't tell you the name of her last album, although I understand that her celebrity derives from her ability to sing and dance. As a child, Britney acted professionally and competed on *Star Search,* distinguishing herself with her surprisingly husky little-girl voice—soon after that, she was famous. I'm sure I've heard Britney's music on the radio without knowing it was her. I usually have a hard time telling pop divas apart because their vocals are so seamlessly produced, and so many of them imitate Britney's coy, breathy style.

It doesn't matter if I like Britney's music, though. Her music is what she does. I love who she *is*.

Britney is one of us.

She's a girl who likes Frappuccinos—who doesn't?

She's a girl who gets thick in the thighs when she doesn't pay attention to her grueling workout schedule. Her body waxes and wanes like any healthy woman's. When she's small, you know she's only a bag of Flamin' Hot Cheetos away from swelling up again. But every lady knows that only corpses and mannequins (and the creepy, spectral Angelina Jolie, who may be one or the other) don't gain weight the week before they bleed. When she's pregnant, Britney tucks into junk food happily, giving the finger to snide journalists who deride her for gaining weight during her confinement (and then for not losing it promptly enough to suit them afterward).

She's a girl famously photographed leaving a gas station rest stop barefoot, her unwashed hair in a simple knot. Who hasn't waited too long to shampoo? Who hasn't said "one more day" in the middle of an impossible workweek, then twisted her hair into a sloppy ponytail to keep the grease and itch at bay? Granted, most of us don't pad into public bathrooms without our shoes, but all the ensuing media hysteria over Brit's grimy feet and lank hair seemed curiously overdone—the contrived outrage merely another way to punish a woman for being dirty in public.

But even the media can't make us un-see the obvious: All externals aside, Britney's fucking *hot*. Britney's healthy, curvy, strong, and feminine. Britney loves to eat, and my guess is she loves to fuck. If sepulchral Angelina Jolie represents the epitome of icy California cool with her virtuous emaciation and her causes and her smart, chic suits, Britney is hot Southern poontang—a girl who isn't afraid to get down and dirty for her own satisfaction no matter what people say, even when their words are meant to annihilate.

Of course she's demonized: Britney is female appetite. Britney *wants*. She wants food and sex and love and trashy, sexy, no-account boys. But it's not the outward manifestation of her appetite her detractors can't abide—after all, many female actresses and singers are heavier than Brit's ever been (Kirstie Alley, Missy Elliott, America Ferrara, Kelly Clarkson, et al.). It's the fact that Britney appears incapable of hiding her appetite the way every woman is taught to from childhood, and whether or not the truth she tells with her body is deliberate, it's undeniably familiar to me and to every single one of my female friends. Every single one of us fights the same war, attempting to forge a tenuous détente between what we want (everything) and what we're supposed to want (nothing). The difference is, Britney's fight is public property. Her attempts to make peace with her own body and its desires are accompanied by a constant chorus of criticism meant to shame and punish. *You* try living with that.

Anna Nicole Smith couldn't. Rest in peace, Vickie Lynn.

DESIRE

Fact: I have a picture of Britney Spears pinned to my wall, right above my desk. It's unposed—clearly a paparazzi photo taken a few years ago during one of her more voluptuous periods. She wears a white dress with cherries printed on it and high wedge sandals that lace around her ankles. The shoes are red, to match the cherries. Her hair is canary yellow, with a defiant black stripe down her center part. She's walking (awkwardly in those high shoes), looking back over her shoulder at someone less famous, a nonentity deliberately cropped out of the frame. Her belly is slightly rounded, and her dancer's legs are thick with muscle. She holds a sweet frozen drink in one hand, straw askew. She's unsmiling, perhaps caught in conversation with her anonymous companion. She's not posing for the camera, though she's clearly aware of it—but in that moment her body is completely hers, not ours. The photographer caught her in a rare moment of breathtaking self-possession. In that photograph, Britney is the most beautiful girl in the world.

I cut out this picture from the magazine as soon as I saw it, cropping out the derisive headline that attempted to humiliate her for her weight and her pretty sundress (apparently, women who aren't skeletal mustn't wear anything with less yardage than a wedding gown). I pinned it to my wall, and I gaze at it often when I'm sitting at my laptop, unable to write. It inspires me to consider the courage it took to put on that cherry-print dress, to lace those shoes, to buy that drink, and to walk into the world boldly to enjoy an afternoon with a friend, as if a million people weren't waiting in the wings to hoot at her, pointing like apes, or to snap her picture and thus profit from another cheap insult at her expense for the sin of having desire.

I danced to "Toxic" ironically, but there's nothing ironic about my love for Britney Spears. I think she's beautiful, but most of all, I think she's brave. I think she's suffered endless humiliation for the crime of growing up—becoming a woman and taking on a woman's struggle. If she'd stayed the same young girl who sang on *Star Search* a lifetime ago—the girl you can still see in very old pictures in which she's dressed like a schoolgirl, hugging her own knees—we'd have no problem with Britney. But now, grown up, manifesting need and want, representing appetite and pleasure, and, worst of all, showing us a female body that reflects a woman's state of mind, we can't stand to look at her; when we do, it'd better be as a hateful joke. Because for most of us (and especially for those of us who make our money by policing women's bodies and minds), the alternative is unthinkable.

I DIDN'T WATCH the MTV Video Music Awards that featured Britney Spears performing her hit "Gimme More." But I saw still pictures from her performance in the magazines I leaf through at the gym. Britney appeared miserable. Her long blond weave looked uncomfortable, and her body language was sheepish and apologetic. Apparently, her lip-synching and dancing weren't sufficiently dazzling to prevent a slew of vicious insults from professional commentators. Her long-awaited comeback was a disaster.

Of course it was. Short of starving herself into a perfectly malleable semblance of womanhood, Britney won't find redemption in showing us more skin. The very words "Gimme More" were tragic misjudgment: We want her to stop wanting so we don't have to think about our own hungers—and whether or not they're being satisfied.

A few weeks ago, Beau brought me a copy of *OK!* magazine with Britney on the cover. (He knows about my obsession and humors me like a good boyfriend should.)

The article was slanderous nonsense, implying that Britney Spears has suffered a psychological break with reality and needs immediate intervention. But it was the pictures I wanted, not the backhanded prose. I clipped out my favorite. It was another paparazzi shot of Britney walking, but in this photograph she wears tall black boots and strides like Colossus, empty-handed and alone. She wears a netted black pillbox hat over lank brown hair. Her arms and legs appear toned and strong, and her face is stony. Her all-black outfit is a defiant claiming of physical territory: *I'll eat what I want, and wear what I want. Fuck all y'all.*

I stared at the photo for a long time then added it to my collection on the wall over my desk: Dark Britney, mysterious and sophisticated, in contrast to all the pictures I have of her as a blonde. But it's her expression that interests me, despite my undeniable attraction to her unusually subdued hair color and her hale femininity. It's the calculating look in her eyes, as if she's finally taking the measure of the world and finding it unacceptably lacking. It's something in the determined set of her unglossed mouth and in the length of her gait, so different from the small awkward steps she took in her red ankle-laced sandals so long ago.

Britney Spears is all grown up, and she's finally pissed off.

And I say it's about fucking time.

WHAT WOULD HAPPEN if we all decided that we were going to eat what we wanted, fuck how we wanted, dress how we wanted, live how we wanted?

What if we decided that we didn't give a shit if someone had a problem with us walking to the store (or into a gas station bathroom) without concealer on our zits or a camera-ready smile plastered across our faces (just in case anybody should be watching us and judging us as insufficiently cheerful)?

What if we stopped pushing our appetites down into tiny little crumpled balls of unmet need and instead unfolded them, smoothed them out with our hands, and then waved them like a banner? Furthermore, what if we *demanded* satisfaction? What if we made our desires *everyone's* problem—a genuine public challenge, like a hurricane or a flood or any other natural phenomenon affecting a large number of human beings?

What if we said, *Hell yeah, I like to eat!* and *Hell yeah, I like to fuck!* and what if we said those things proudly, to everyone, instead of whispering them shamefully into our best friend's ear late at night after too many glasses of red wine?

What if we admitted that women's bodies—*our* bodies—want sex and pleasure and food and that we'd rather have a good meal and wear fat pants the next day than spend an extra half hour at the gym, peeling our bodies away incrementally? What if we danced because we wanted to, for the sheer pleasure of it, without being concerned that our moves aren't provocative enough?

And what if Britney Spears shaved her head because she was sick of spending endless hours getting fussed over, primped and poked into everybody else's idea of how she was supposed to look? What if she was sick of living in a world in which she was expected to betray her own physical needs in order to keep other women in line? What if she just woke up one day and thought, *Fuck it—just fuck it,* and went to McDonald's for a sausage-and-egg biscuit and a Coke, and when the paparazzi started taking pictures of her for the obligatory "Britney—Obese and Depressed" articles, what if she stopped and said, "You know what? I'm rich enough to eat what I want," and gave them all the finger?

What if, instead of buying the magazines that call Britney Spears crazy and ugly and fat and drug-addicted, a bad mother and a slut—magazines funded by the beauty and diet industries, by the way, two conglomerates not known for their respect for women in general—what if we spent that time figuring out what we really wanted and how to get it? What if some of us liked Britney's music and bought her CDs and others of us didn't care for it and didn't buy them, but what if we left Britney's body out of the equation? Does her *voice* get fat? Do we need to know how much she's working out before we can enjoy her latest single?

Do we really like watching Britney be pilloried for being the same as us, a real woman with physical appetite?

Or are we scared that if we don't actively add to her public humiliation, someone will notice that we have desires ourselves?

I GET THE strong feeling Britney Spears is about to tell us all to fuck off. The head-shaving was a pretty clear message. So are the tall black boots and her new, loose-armed strut. I like this Britney a lot, and I anticipate her explosion with a great deal of hope. If anyone can pull this off, it's Britney.

Not Madonna. Not Courtney.

It's Britney, bitch.

Fried Chicken Interlude: Picnic Style

☠

FRYING CHICKEN IS A WILD, FERAL ACT OF MEAT-LOVING debauchery involving bone and skin and sizzling fat and juices running pink to clear as the body parts of what used to be a living, individual bird cook to the point of succulence. If that's not cool with you, go buy a box of McNuggets instead and skip this chapter. (I suspect that McNuggets are made with so little actual chicken that they may qualify as vegan.)

Get some chicken. Bone in, skin on. None of that sanitized *boneless, skinless* shit. Don't bother.

Free range? If you must. Antibiotic-free? Whatever floats your boat. Personally, I wait until chicken parts go on sale for under $1 a pound at the supermarket, then I buy as much as I can afford and freeze what I don't want to use immediately. But that's just me, and I'm poor. And I'm all for people doing what they need to do, and if spending your hard-earned sourdough on fancy grain-fed boutique chickens is what you need to do then so be it. Just make sure you're getting chicken parts that include bone and skin—because even designer chickens still have those proletarian qualities, regardless of how upscale their diet and how lush their accommodations.

Bone and skin flavor meat. Yes, the presence of bone and skin reminds us that something we'd like to serve for dinner used to be a living creature. But if you're not at peace with your meat-eating—if you can only stand to eat boneless, skinless chicken cutlets, processed and sanitized from actual chicken body parts into fatless jellied pucks resembling saline breast implants—then I respectfully suggest not attempting to fry chicken at home.

But if you're "down with the sickness," to borrow a phrase from the nice boys in the band Disturbed—if you're at peace or at least in détente with your own savagery—if your mouth waters at the idea of ripping and tearing a certain luscious, once-living something apart—then get some chicken parts, file your canine teeth into points, and let's rock this bitch.

Because I think "the sickness" tastes mighty fine.

CHICKEN PARTS: bone in, skin on.

Rinse the chicken under cool water and pat it dry with paper towels.

You can soak the chicken pieces in milk or buttermilk over-night if you have a bunch of milk on hand and no pressing need for fried chicken *right now*. Soaking the chicken makes the meat juicier, it's true; but if you're on a budget it can be hard to justify throwing away that much milk after the raw chicken parts finish their spa treatment. I only soak my chicken when I'm trying really, really hard to cook someone into bed with my good-time, down-home culinary mojo, and in that situation the difference between good chicken and *great* chicken might mean the difference between going to bed alone and going to bed with a buttermilk-biscuit-dazed paramour eager to sample the fare below *my* Mason-Dixon line. But if I'm not cooking to seduce, my chicken goes without the benefit of a milk bath. Southern hospitality is one thing, but throwing away a half-gallon of milk every time I want a pan of fried bird parts is just faulty home economics.

Once you've patted the chicken pieces dry (of water or of milk), dip them into a bowl of two or three beaten eggs (if you like your fried chicken batter a little heavier). I do this sometimes, and other times I don't. The thing about a recipe for fried chicken is that it contains multitudes: It can be prepared about a million different ways, and all of them are good. Milk or buttermilk or no milk, egg or not: It's up to you. Ultimately, you're gonna have a damn good pan of fried chicken on your hands no matter what.

Dump the egged (or not egged) chicken parts into a plastic grocery bag. Make sure the bag is intact, or, if you're paranoid, you can double-bag. If you have a gallon-size Ziploc bag, by all means, use it.

Here are some things to throw into the bag on top of the chicken in various proportions, depending on what you have in your kitchen:

- white flour

- cornmeal

FRIED CHICKEN INTERLUDE

- leftover cornbread, crumbled up very fine

- potato chips, smashed into near-powder; any flavor works, but barbecue chips add a certain je ne sais quoi

- saltine, Ritz, Waverly, or any other crackers, similarly crushed into tiny bits

- store-bought bread crumbs

- Corn Flakes[1]

It's a good idea to add at least *some* white flour—maybe half flour, half whatever else you're using—because the flour is fine enough to get in all the nooks and crannies of your chicken parts, preventing unappetizing piebald bare spots. If you don't have anything else *but* white flour, that's okay too. Sometimes—and I say this honestly—the simplest fried chicken is the best. Sometimes a light flour coating is all you need and all you could ever imagine wanting. I'm just throwing in some options so if you feel like getting all fancy—or if you have stuff in your kitchen cupboards you want to use up—you can.

Along with the flour (and whatever else you're using, if you're using any ingredients from the bulleted list), add a whole lot of ground black pepper, about a teaspoon of baking powder, a generous spoonful of paprika (if you have it—I almost never do, but it adds color and subtle flavor), what will seem like way too much salt (but, in reality, is probably not even enough), and two spoonfuls of garlic powder. You can also toss in a few spoonfuls of each (or none) of the following: poultry seasoning,

---

1. I've never tried this because I don't tend to buy cereal, but a few folks swear by crushed Corn Flakes in their fried chicken batter. And who am I to scoff?

Cajun or Creole seasoning, rosemary, marjoram, thyme, white pepper, Trappey's Red Devil Sauce, Tabasco sauce, or whatever else you have around the kitchen that you think would go well with chicken. Stick your nose in the bag and inhale. Does the batter smell like the kind of fried chicken you want? If not, keep adding seasonings and adjust the proportions. Add more salt. Add more black pepper.

Once your batter smells the way you think it should, close the top of the plastic bag(s) and shake the chicken until every piece is completely coated.

Now, heat a skillet to just over medium heat on your range. Cast-iron is best, of course, but if you don't have a cast-iron skillet just use your biggest, deepest frying pan. Throw in enough shortening so that when it melts it's about half an inch deep. (Yes, that will be a lot of shortening.) If you have any bacon fat, add a few spoonfuls of that to the shortening to flavor it, but don't fry your chicken in 100 percent bacon fat because it will end up tasting a bit burned, I've found. Bacon fat is fairly delicate—it works better as a flavoring agent than as an actual workhorse fat like shortening or lard.

Test the temperature of the melted shortening by flicking a few drops of water from your fingertips into the pan. If the water droplets sizzle and appear to hop around, you're good to go. Don't flick too hard—you don't want an eyeful of hot Crisco. Trust me on that—it stings worse than come (not that that's ever happened to me—no, sir).

Turn your oven on to 375 degrees.

Now, carefully put the first pieces of chicken into the hot oil. Carefully! Use tongs! Because the last thing you want is a bunch

FRIED CHICKEN INTERLUDE

of hot oil splashing up and burning you! Don't crowd the chicken pieces in the skillet—give them plenty of room so the hot fat can circulate around each piece freely. Use tongs (or a fork) to turn each piece over frequently, and fry until the skin is golden brown (about ten to fifteen minutes total). Remove the fried chicken to an oven-safe baking pan (the long rectangular kind used for sheet cakes works best—9 x 12 or so).

Fry the next batch of chicken till golden brown, and add those pieces to the baking pan. You'll need to add more shortening to the skillet as you continue frying.

Keep going until all your chicken parts are fried and in the pan. Grind more black pepper over the pieces, shake on more salt, and sprinkle on more Trappey's or Tabasco sauce, if you like. If you want your chicken to look extra pretty, sprinkle some of the herbs you used to flavor the batter on top.

Pop the pan in the oven, uncovered. Cook for about fifteen minutes—wings get done faster, and breasts take the longest. Check to see if the chicken is done all the way through by cutting through a chicken breast to the bone—if the juices run clear instead of pink, it's done. If not, leave in for another five to ten minutes.

If you don't want to cook your chicken in the oven, just keep frying it in batches on your stove-top till the skin is golden brown and the meat is cooked through, turning each piece often. I like the oven method, though, because that way all my chicken is ready to be served at once.

Remove the pan from your oven and drain the chicken pieces on plates covered in paper towels. Eat with fingers as soon as the fried chicken is cool enough to touch. Serve with biscuits and homemade apricot jam or cream gravy if you're trying to get laid, or with Wonder Bread and margarine (or corn fritters) if you're feeling authentic. Don't bother with a tossed green salad. Nobody in their right mind would eat salad when they could have another piece of fried chicken! The only thing green on the table should be collards, which are easy enough to prepare and which don't really count as vegetables, since they're really only delivery systems for more salt and pork fat.

But really, your chicken will stand alone. Be proud of it. Eat it until you're talking like Foghorn Leghorn. This is the payoff for all your hard work. And any date worth ten minutes of your time will match you piece for piece.

Have plenty of paper towels on the table, you bone-in, skin-on lovebirds. You'll want 'em. Good fried chicken—like excellent sex—is invariably messy, and usually involves a fair amount of finger-licking.

HERE'S THE BEST thing about fried chicken: No matter how good it is freshly made out of the oven, *it's even better the next day*, cold from the fridge. My Oklahoma-born grandmother delicately refers to cold next-day fried chicken as "picnic-style," and that seems about right to me, even though the last time I went to a park and ate on a blanket I was bitten by sand mites and panhandled relentlessly.

But still—*picnic-style:* a red-checkered blanket, a basket, two wine glasses, a plate of fresh, cool grapes. A gracious old tree, providing shade! A cloudless blue sky! And grass cropped as neatly as a golf course beneath your blanket as you and your lover reach into the picnic basket and seize pieces of fried chicken. Then, baring your teeth like wild dogs and grunting in sheer animal pleasure, you greedily rip muscle from bone as the grease slicks your chin.

Well, *I* find it romantic.

II.
FLESH

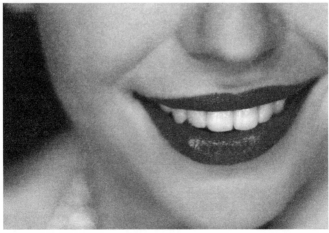

INTRODUCTION

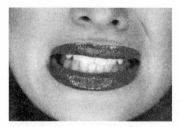

WHEN MY EDITRESS SENT ME THE FIRST ROUND OF MOCK-UPS for the cover of this book, I was greatly dismayed.

One cover showed a very, very slender woman from the rear standing in front of a kitchen sink. The focal point of the image was her fist-size bottom, showcased by sexy black lace panties. Her bare back made it clear she was topless. The knobs of her spine cast shadows on her skin. "Sex and Bacon" trilled the title underneath her derriere in unironic contrast to the woman's starved appearance.

It wasn't the idea of having a naked lady on my cover that upset me. After all, my first book had one—and Lord, how I loved it when the audiences I read to asked me if it was *my* hot booty (instead of a professional model's) on the cover! ("No," I'd answer demurely, as if splaying my ass on a product meant for public consumption was a completely alien concept to me, despite the fact that you can see my actual ass*hole* on any number of pornographic websites for free.)

So, no, it wasn't seeing a naked lady in sexy undies on my book cover, her bottom centered right above the title, that bothered me. Naked ladies are my bread and butter, as I've been one for pay, and write about ones I've known and loved. It wasn't even the fact that most of her head and her legs were cropped away as nonessential, like the parts of an animal you don't care to eat.

The model's stripped-down angularity was the opposite of everything I wanted my book to be about. I was writing about good food, hot sex, the mystery and beauty of women's bodies, and my cover showed a woman who looked like her last meal was sometime during the first Bush regime. She was so thin her shoulders were wider than her hips. How would you go about fucking a woman like that? You'd break her in half like a Hummel figurine trying to get inside her. I imagined trying to spread her bloodless thighs and hearing the sound of her pelvic girdle cracking apart. She had no padding, no protection, no *flesh*. Despite the racy lingerie, she was as sexless as a houseplant.

I wrote and discarded several emails to my editress in response to the cover image she'd asked me to consider. Finally, I wrote, *If we're going to use a woman's body on the cover of this book, can we at least pick a model who looks like she both eats* and *fucks?*

I imagined an alternate image: a thick, sleek otter of a woman, rounded and grinning, posed from the front so you could see all the personality and individuality of her face. I saw her leaning against the sink with her arms crossed sassily, a plate

INTRODUCTION

of cake parked next to one gorgeous thigh. I dressed her in the same lacy black panties, but all of a sudden they were way too sexy—almost obscene—so I replaced them with well-worn, fitted jeans that were erotic in a different way, speaking to a woman's comfort in her own kitchen and her pleasure in filling her belly with a sweet treat, simply for its own sake. I left her shirt off—her crossed arms covering her breasts for modesty's sake—and imagined her stomach, a strong convex arc.

Now that's *the proper image for a book about sex and food,* I thought approvingly. A woman who evidently takes pleasure in both eating and fucking—a lady who personifies Appetite, and has the flesh to prove it.

When I sent my suggestions for a more appropriate cover image back to my publisher, my objections were taken seriously. The art department ended up bagging the whole "anonymous, naked fashion model in the kitchen" idea. Instead, the new cover featured *me*—scantily clad in my own real-life kitchen, brandishing my favorite cast-iron skillet. My bluff had been summarily called: *You want a picture of a woman who eats and fucks? You got it, babe!* When I saw the new cover mock-up, I couldn't stop laughing. I loved it.

I figure if you're going to use the image of a nearly nude female to sell a product, the most honorable way to slum is to at least use your own damn body, in all its quirky imperfection, instead of paying another woman to drop her drawers for you. So, after over a decade of peeling off my clothes for strangers, I'm finally putting my own flesh on the line for this book. I wrote it and that's my real, live, chubby, bacon-loving body on the cover. On a book cataloguing my appetites in obsessive, slobbering, and occasionally disgusting detail, anyone who wants to can look at my flesh and form their own opinions— and that seems about right to me.

"LAMB," "THE BACON Quotient," "Red Gravy," and "Forbidden Fruit" are about my unquenchable lust for flesh. "Red Gravy" was one of the first pieces I wrote for this book, and "Forbidden Fruit" was one of the last.

"Thin" and "Fat" are about our attempts to control our bodies.

And "Host" poses the question *What's eating you?*

Throw a big, bloody steak on the grill and enjoy.

LAMB

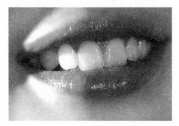

IT'S FINALLY FALL, AFTER A LONG, MISERABLE SUMMER
during which Seattle resembled Los Angeles more than any sea-
going city ever should. The rains haven't started yet, but I look
forward to them. The city still stinks of summer: hot pavement,
dog shit, dying grass, and the exhaust fumes of a million stalled
vehicles. We need rain to wash our poor city clean. As an added
benefit, the rain will put a six-month damper on all outdoor activities and the sporty people who enjoy them. While the Frisbee-
tossers stay in and nurse their seasonal affective disorder, the
city becomes mine again. I look forward to endless urban hikes
wrapped in my big wool coat. I don't even mind the obligatory
rain jokes that must be tolerated for the sake of municipal order.

I'm a grouch and I don't like summer at all. The dreariness of fall suits me just fine, thank you very much. I'm at my best when the days are short. I love the sun when it's just a silver coin high in the sky, shedding little heat and less light. I love bundling up, wearing scarves and gloves and sweaters and multiple pairs of socks. Everyone's so much more attractive in cold-weather clothing—the lines of their bodies are smoothed out and their flaws are concealed. You can look at them and imagine anything you like.

Most of all, though, I love the food of autumn.

I have a lamb roast in the refrigerator, marinating in olive oil, balsamic vinegar, and handfuls and handfuls of both garlic and oregano. Though lamb is a paschal food, meant to be eaten in the spring, I intend to hunker down, bundle up, and roast my lamb in a low, slow oven.

I plan on leaving the lamb roast to marinate for a few days, turning it every twenty-four hours or so. By the time I put it into my oven, it'll be so tender it'll fall apart at the merest whisper of fork-pressure. The long, slow roasting will transform the surface of the meat into a savory crust that will protect the cool pink interior from becoming overly done, resulting in slices of lamb that are crisp and salty on the outside and meltingly silky on the inside. I'll cook the lamb with small white potatoes, which will become coated with lamb drippings as they bake. I could eat potatoes cooked with drippings all day and never even miss the meat.

Autumn food also means pumpkin bread, pumpkin pie, pumpkin mousse, and pumpkin soup. Pumpkin everything. I do love cooked pumpkin, with its beta-carotene and its virtuous fiber. I love it sweet, I love it savory, I even like it carved up into jack-o'-lanterns. I never thought I'd have so much affection for a gourd.

Autumn food is all about roasting, slow-cooking, stewing, and simmering. Autumn food is about patience. When the days are short and your apartment's freezing, a warm oven can be your hearth. Why spend your home time chilly and miserable in your living room? A cozy kitchen can be your base of operations. Invite your friends in, get them half-drunk on hearty red wine, and feed them.

FLESH

THIN

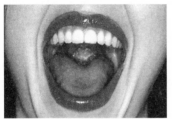

I HAVE A FRIEND WITH AN EATING DISORDER. IN ABOUT
nine months I watched her shrink from a healthy size 16 to a
loose-skinned size 4. She has no plans to stop until she reaches
the Mecca toward which all anorexics point and pray five times
a day: size 0. When she reaches 0, she says, she'll stop. When she
can wear toddler-size jeans, she says, she'll finally feel thin.

The idea of child-size jeans with absurdly long, adult-
woman-length legs makes me think of christening gowns. All that
fussy white lace cascading nearly to the floor! Should she reach
size 0 and decide to marry, my friend could slip into a christening
gown just as easily as a wedding dress, and nobody would be the
wiser. Maybe that's what anorexics really want: a second crack at
the clothes they wore as infants.

Meanwhile, my friend's skin is craterous and her hair is dull and, worst of all, she lost her weight strangely: Her arms and legs are pipe-cleaner thin and her poor pitted face is gaunt, making her teeth and tongue appear far too large for her head, but the tiny amount of body fat she does carry wraps around her hips and lower belly like an inner tube, giving her a bottom-heavy look despite her emaciation. She waddles when she walks: Her knees barely kiss, and there's a vast whistling triangular gap between her thighs where muscle and fat should be. Her inner tube of flesh swings from side to side awkwardly with every step.

I imagine her body causes her much distress. I picture her standing in front of her full-length mirror every night determined to *keep starving.* I think of her pinching the skin of her belly and hips and ass viciously, wishing it all away. And honestly, it's the fat around her middle that's probably keeping her from being a size 0 already. Without it she'd have the torso of a toddler. A *thin* toddler. Then maybe she could finally stop.

At size 16 she was sleek and sexy, a big healthy horse of a girl, all strong flank and firm, high ass. She was toned. She *rippled.* She didn't realize how hot she was: Men and women watched her longingly. Now she fucks boys who are willing to overlook her appearance, or who are able to eroticize it as insectile, dangerous, alien. At least I hope that's what they're doing when they bend her over and fuck her, staring down at the bumpy knobs of her spine. I hope they're not fantasizing about toddlers in snap-crotch jeans or infants in christening gowns.

Since losing so much weight, my friend is frail and easily tires. I catch her staring at my thighs and belly with fascination, the way we sneak peeks at amputees and burn victims and ex-

FLESH

tremely obese people riding Rascals. When we eat together she counts my bites. I've caught her mentally measuring my girth and shaking her head at my unapologetic fleshiness. *A double-digit dress size! Better to be dead than that fat ever again!*

Today i ate an apple and half a subway sandwich, she emailed me. *that's it!*

"Today I ate pancakes and sausage for breakfast, chicken teriyaki for lunch, and a big beet salad for dinner," I wrote back. "I had a slice of fresh, homemade raspberry crumble pie for dessert."

I didn't hear from her again for two weeks. I suppose the raspberry pie was unforgivable.

Which is not to say that I never feel fat and never make an effort to slim down. When my clothes start feeling tight, I make a few concessions: I'll bake my fish instead of frying it, and I'll have fruit and yogurt for breakfast instead of French toast. I drink more water and less alcohol, and I try to work in a few more visits to the gym. At my smallest, I'm a size 10. At my heaviest, I'm a 12. That range feels about right to me. I have no idea what I weigh.

I have a real problem with anorexia. I can't help seeing it as internalized misogyny.

The thing is, women are supposed to be woman-shaped. Our thighs are supposed to touch. We're at our best when we're healthy, strong, soft, and libidinous. We're at our most fuckable when we're well-fed and sleek, not when we're dry as toast and out of our minds with hunger. So if you want to get a little more toned, remember—everything you put in your mouth should bring you pleasure and feed your beautiful curves, whether it's lard-fried chicken or an abstemious bite of salad. Being hungry and miserable is never okay. Hunger makes women mean and dumb, and Lord knows we need all our wits about us just to exist in this world as thinking, feeling, art-creating women. If we're too hungry to think, we're too hungry to fuck shit up. If we're too hungry to fuck shit up, we're collaborating with the enemy.

That means: *Eat real food.* Foods labeled "low-cal," "fat-free," "sugar-free," "diet," or—God forbid—"lite," are like fake orgasms: They look just like real food, but they don't satisfy. If you want something low-cal, fat-free, and sugar-free, eat a carrot. Chemicals are no substitute for nutrients.

One of my favorite weapons in the battle I like to call "Operation: Get Less Fat!" are those big bags of boneless, skinless chicken breasts you find in the frozen section of any big grocery store. Throw a bag of chicken breasts into your freezer, and when you're hungry, simply defrost a few pieces, bake them at 400 degrees for about twenty to twenty-five minutes, and voila—good clean-burning protein with nary a "lite" in sight.

Of course nobody likes plain, unseasoned chicken. So try some of the following before baking:

- Rub your chicken with a little olive oil. Mince a few cloves of garlic (or, if you're like me, use a couple of spoonfuls of bottled preminced garlic or garlic paste from a tube). Massage the garlic into the chicken and finish with a generous dusting of both salt and pepper.

- Marinate the chicken in your favorite vinaigrette salad dressing for twenty-four hours, turning once.

- Mix up equal portions of soy sauce, honey, and canola or olive oil. Add a generous spoonful of garlic and another spoonful of ground ginger. Add a splash

FLESH

of lemon juice. You can either marinate the chicken in this mixture for a day or you can just brush it on both sides and bake it immediately (though the flavor will be stronger and richer if you let your chicken soak overnight).

• Make a sauce of plain yogurt and dill. Put some on the chicken before baking, and keep some in the refrigerator to use as a dip once your chicken is cooked. Slice the breasts into strips, dip them into the cool yogurt-dill, and eat them with your fingers. Better yet, let someone feed you.

• Rub the chicken breasts with a little butter. Sprinkle them with a generous amount of dried rosemary and a little thyme. Finish with salt and pepper. The butter will make your chicken brown beautifully, and the rosemary will make your whole house smell delicious.

The possibilities of chicken are endless: It's like good old penis-in-vagina sex—there are a million ways to do it, from missionary to superfreaky, and all of them get the job done.

Feed yourself protein, then go out and fuck shit up. You'll be surprised at how beautiful that makes you feel.

WHEN I WAS working as a lingerie model at Butterscotch's, I was often scheduled with a Chicago debutante who came to Seattle for the drugs. She smoked crack to keep her weight down and took Ecstasy in lieu of high-calorie cocktails when she went

81

out. She was tall and whippet-thin, with concave shanks and a completely visible rib cage. She looked like an anatomical drawing of the skeletal system come to life. A few fetish-oriented customers loved her, but most preferred curvier models. When she danced, she looked like a marionette being bounced on its own strings.

Bear this in mind: As physically wasted as my coworker was, even *she* wasn't a size 0. When even a crack habit won't make you as thin as a Hollywood starlet or a fashion model, it's time to reevaluate the beauty standards that keep us literally starving ourselves to death.

A NOTE ON VEGETABLES

Vegetables are tricky—I'll admit it. They've always seemed like a lot of work to me, without the commensurate payoff. Making a cake from scratch is a lot of work, too, but at the end of the process you have a whole cake, and cake is delicious!

But when you fix vegetables, all you get are . . . vegetables. And unless you're a radical vegan, veggies aren't much of a treat.

The thing that keeps me from veggie-love is, frankly, laziness. I think I have Food ADHD: I like food that's ready for me when *I'm* ready for *it*—and if it's delicious and fancy in some way, that's even better! If it's brightly colored or makes noise or there are lit sparklers stuck in it, even better! *Ka-POW!* Vegetables, on the other hand, are as subtle and reserved as an Ingmar Bergman flick. For someone with a fairly aggressive internal sense of editing, there's just not enough going on with vegetables to bother.

The whole process is laborious: First you have to pick them out, selecting the individual vegetable or vegetables you plan to serve later. There's no uniformity—you have to look over each vegetable for freshness and lack of damage, and usually you end up putting a dozen back before you find one worthy specimen. Then you have to take them home, wash them, and, in some cases, peel them. You have to cut parts of them off. Then, finally, you cook and eat them. By that time I'm usually pretty sick of the vegetable in question, and I've usually ordered Domino's and filled up on Cheesy Bread.

So what I've figured out with vegetables is that you have to act *fast*, before you give up and call for takeout. That's why veggies like asparagus are good: They require very little processing to become edible and reasonably tasty—unlike, say, artichokes or spaghetti squash.

Broccoli's another fast-acting veggie. So are green beans.

Just take the vegetables of your choice, wash them, and cut off their ends. Toss them into a metal steamer, and fit the steamer into a pot with a couple inches of boiling water in the bottom. Make sure the water level is *below* the bottom of the steamer: You're steaming your veggies, not boiling them.

Put the lid on the pot and allow the water to continue boiling for about seven minutes. Check your vegetables by poking them with a fork. If the fork goes in with only a little resistance, your veggies are ready to eat. If not, close the lid and steam for a few more minutes.

Once your vegetables are steamed, put them on a plate and drizzle them with a little olive oil and some balsamic vinegar, or with the flavored vinegar of your choice (raspberry is a favorite of mine), or with lemon juice, or with whatever salad dressing you have on hand. A little salt and pepper will add flavor. You can stick sparklers in them if you want. They're not quite *ka-*

POW!, but if you're trying to get a little sleeker (and you're not nursing a crack habit or an eating disorder), sometimes you have to pick vegetables over cake.

Luckily, not often.

LOSING WEIGHT SHOULDN'T be a painful proposition: Think *spa*, not *labor camp*.

Think about simple food, served elegantly: one perfect pear, sliced and fanned on a bed of fresh greens; a handful of strawberries, cleaned and hulled, served chilled in your favorite tea cup; a steak, grilled or pan-fried to perfection, served with freshly ground sea salt.

The important thing is that you're eating until you feel satisfied, and that everything you eat is delicious. Take walks through your local farmers market, buying the plumpest, juiciest-looking produce you can find. Have histrionic sex marathons with your partner, changing positions often. Drink lots of water, but make sure you're having it restaurant-style, in a glass with ice and a straw and a slice of lemon.

Let your beautiful body find its own stasis.

Don't *ever* starve yourself.

THE BACON QUOTIENT

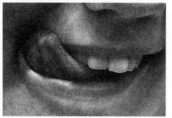

THERE'S NEVER ENOUGH BACON.

When you go to a restaurant and order breakfast you usually only receive three or four measly little strips bookended by far too much toast and a greasy mound of semiraw hash browns. Even ordering an additional side of bacon only makes six or eight strips, total. And these are strips the size of Band-Aids, carbonized into chalky blackened mouthfuls of bacon-flavored charcoal briquette! So not only do you not get enough bacon in restaurants, you generally don't feel satisfied by the bacon you're having. The whole thing's disappointing. You might as well order the fruit and yogurt plate. It's not like you're going to feel good about your breakfast anyway.

I was sick of never getting enough quality bacon. So one

day, I decided to see how much bacon would be enough. I knew it was definitely more than four strips, and almost certainly more than eight. I knew the bacon would have to be good. I was pretty sure *enough* bacon would be a *lot*.

The thing was, I had the day off. Not much to do. I had a big unopened package of bacon in the refrigerator and a cast-iron skillet on my range-top, scrubbed out and seasoned with oil. It seemed like if I was ever going to find out how much bacon was enough, the only way to get at that knowledge would be to simply start frying strips of pork in my pan. To eat. And then to stop, once the crucial bacon quotient—the BQ—had been achieved. It would be elegant, a simple Scientific Method two-step. I considered taking notes, then decided the note-taking would interfere with my experience of the project. I needed to be able to pay attention. The BQ could be a subtle point, easily missed. I couldn't afford to take that chance.

I started out with a cold pan on my stove-top. I laid five strips of bacon across the bottom of the pan, pushing them together with a fork, neat and flat, into broad pink-and-white pork ribbons. They were slightly too long for the pan, and their edges curled up on each side. I was mildly annoyed by the crimped edges—it didn't look precise—but I used my fork to press the too-long edges against the sides of the skillet, and they adhered with their own fat quite nicely. It would have to do.

I turned the burner on to medium-high. Actually, just past medium. There's a certain bacon-friendly setting my hand knows better than my brain, because if I just kind of flick the knob in a certain way it goes to Perfect Bacon Temperature and my bacon cooks into delicious salty crusty strips of goodness. But if I overthink the temperature my pan ends up too hot or too cool. So with a twist of the wrist, loose and casual, in about three minutes the bacon started to creak as the brine in which it had been packed burned off against the hot cast iron.

About a minute after that I smelled it. The bacon smell. That rich, caramelized scent of sizzling salt-pork belly. That *unfair* smell. The one that tells you that a double order—bacon with your starch-heavy meal, plus another side of bacon—isn't enough. The one that vegetarians shamefully make allowances for, asking for bacon in restaurants while maintaining pristinely meat-free homes.

Each strip's fatty sections swelled and curled coyly in the pan, making seductive popping noises. *Shhhhhhh,* the bacon whispered, promising discretion. I was hungry and excited, an ardent lover. Finally, enough bacon! I couldn't wait for the first batch to finish.

I opened my cabinet and took out a dinner plate, which I lined with a double layer of paper towels. Then I speared each strip of bacon with my fork and laid them side by side on their paper towel bed. I finished by gently tucking another paper towel over the bacon strips, as if wishing them a good night's rest and pleasant dreams. Grease-flowers blossomed as I pressed the towel down, careful as a mama seeing to her babies.

Turning back to the grease-coated skillet, I used my fingers to lay five more strips down. I believe in touching bacon. I am a meat-toucher. Don't get me wrong—I wouldn't use raw meat to clean my countertops, and I wouldn't lick uncooked pork or suck the drippings from those weird little sanitary napkin thingies they put under cut-up fryers in the Styrofoam trays to absorb the smelly chicken water. But I believe in touching meat—using my fingers to lay down bacon or dredge chunks of stew meat in flour. If meat were really that dangerous, wouldn't we all be sick constantly from eating it? Frankly, it seemed to me that supermarket mushrooms—raised in shit, then dumped out into trays to be pawed through by dozens of indifferently washed shoppers—were likely filthier than nice, clean meat wrapped in butcher's plastic and consistently refrigerated.

Or maybe I just liked touching meat. The cool slap of it and the soft meat-grease on my fingertips. The smell of it—feral, coppery, intimate, oily. The watery blood. The raw animal-meat-fiber striations of beef; smooth, shiny egg-yolky chicken breasts; even the little worms of raw ground beef were sensual in their own way when you slapped them into hamburger-size pads or used your fingers to squish eggs and cracker crumbs and ketchup into meatloaves. So I used my fingers to lay the next series of bacon strips down, peeling them away from the main block of candy-striped meat with my nails.

This time they began crackling and pushing up into little pork bumps and valleys immediately—the salty water hissing, the grease from the previous batch spattering slightly—and I felt pinpricks of hot oil on my hands and forearms. I welcomed the tiny splashes of pain. They didn't hurt badly. I licked my wrist, cooling the burn there and tasting exquisite bacon essence in the drop of hot fat on my tongue. I rinsed my hands perfunctorily.

Turning to the nest of sleeping bacon on my counter, I cruelly plucked off their greasy paper towel coverlet. Incited to violence by the brief flutter of bacon fat I'd lapped from my own wrist, I crammed an entire strip of cooked bacon into my mouth. And another. And another. Standing, I gobbled bacon. Bits of browned

FLESH

pork fell from my lips to the floor. I was doing it! I was doing the experiment! I was finding the BQ!

I ate silently and rapidly until all five strips were gone. Then I used a licked finger to get the tiny fragments of bacon stuck to the paper towel, pressing my fingertips into the greasy bed and licking the particles from my own living, uncharred skin. It was so *good*.

I gazed lustfully at the bacon in the skillet, half-done and seductively disarrayed, dressed in the hot fat of the pan's previous occupancy.

Using my fork, I speared each strip and flipped each one over, arranging them into a neat, straight chorus line of sizzling pork. I used the tines of my fork to press the white nodules of pig fat firmly against the hot iron interior of the pan. The rich, silky veins of fat snapped and seared brown as the pink meat of the bacon contracted and darkened similarly. It was beautiful, like watching a flower burst open in stop-motion cinematography. The aroma of bacon hung in the air maddeningly.

After a few minutes, I moved the second five strips of bacon from the skillet to the plate of paper towels. I didn't bother covering them with another towel. This batch was a mite overdone. Besides, I didn't think they'd last long enough to appreciate my solicitude. They lay on the plate naked and stacked against each other. And that *smell*. It was engorging, inciting. It was as if the first plate of bacon were merely an appetizer. The second was the entrée. The meat of the matter, so to speak.

I carried the plate to the table. Sat. Gobbled bacon. The plate was empty before I settled into my chair. Which was fine, because I really needed to start the third pan of bacon. I got up again and

89

returned to the range, casually arranging another layer of paper towels on top of the first two grease-sodden ones.

I realized I felt happy—really happy. I hadn't had enough bacon, not yet—but I was on the track of my BQ, and that felt good. And I still had more than half a package of raw bacon left. For that matter, I had another whole package in the freezer. It would be short work to defrost it under warm running water, if it came to that. I sang as I laid five more strips in the pan of lightly smoking oil.

I fried and ate bacon for two and a half hours in a back-and-forth ballet among range, countertop, and table. My feet slid along the floor noiselessly—I was grease-skating in my socks, gliding like a swan. With every breath I inhaled slippery clouds of bacon fat, transformed into a smoky haze by the alchemy of my cast-iron skillet and the heat of my stove-top. I was in the fat and the fat was in me, all over me, deep in my creases like a tender lover. Inner had become outer. It was all the same. It was glorious and sinful, a gluttonous greasy rampage, a disaster, a glistening salty triumph.

The BQ was technically reached at three pounds (uncooked weight), but I made sure to eat the remaining pound in the package just to ensure the accuracy of my results. I didn't want to be mistaken—to *think* that I'd reached the BQ, only to realize an hour later that I'd been premature. I had to be *sure*. The last pound of bacon was deliberate and labored, but at long last I finished cooking and devouring the entire family-size four-pound package. I folded the greasy plastic wrapping into quarters and discarded it into my kitchen garbage can, replacing the lid with a sense of completion and purpose. I was done. I had finally had Enough Bacon.

90

FLESH

HOST

I AM SOMETIMES IRRATIONALLY CERTAIN THAT I HAVE A
tapeworm. Or some other form of intestinal parasite—I'm
not picky.

By *sometimes* I mean *frequently,* if by *frequently* you understand
that I mean my colonic hyperconsciousness is a gentle, unceasing
drone in the background of my own specific mental soundtrack—
sometimes nearly inaudible and sometimes thunderous—but always *there,* constantly pulsing in counterpoint to the tidal thump
and slide of my own heartbeat.[1] I am obsessed with the idea that
my body might be the unwitting host for colonies of alien life,
flourishing without my knowledge in some dark intestinal nook
or cranny. I can't stop thinking about what I would do if I learned

---

1. I do realize there are medications specifically designed to address this problem.

I was infected. My first inclination would be to drink something caustic, like lye. Sure, I'd die, but at least the worms would too! I'd die *clean,* by God!

Let me back up.

About ten years ago I dated a woman who was employed as a Colonic Irrigationist[2] at an alternative health center.

Her job was pretty much exactly what her title implied: She spent the day putting plastic tubes up people's asses and sluicing out their lower intestines with various quantities of sodium-balanced warm water, with the aim of loosening any impacted feces stuck to the sides of their intestinal walls like the calcium scales that clog hard-water plumbing. Sometimes those shit deposits were benign, but other times they contained parasites—bugs and worms that got into her clients' bodies via undercooked fish or meat, or by too-intimate contact with their infected pets' waste. Fancy, spidery parasites could be obtained through adventurous eating during travel in certain developing countries, though some were absorbed through the skin during hiking or wading through brackish water. But ordinarily—barring foreign travel—most people just had worms. Plain, ordinary, everyday worms.

"Like dogs and cats," my girlfriend informed me earnestly. "They usually look like grains of white rice."

That knowledge did not add to my comfort (or to my previously uncomplicated enjoyment of rice). So many Americans walking around with worm eggs and tapeworms in their lower intestines, munching away happily on Big Macs and Frappuccinos, shedding portions of their unwanted guests' bodies in their

---

2. And yes, I do understand that many porno movies start with this exact exposition, but trust me, this isn't that kind of essay.

FLESH

own healthy turds! How could you live with yourself, knowing you were infected? Worse, how could you live *not knowing?* You'd think you were clean—you could shower, wear fresh underwear, floss, and eat organic produce—but all along, underneath all the health and wholesomeness, your guts would be *curdling with worms*. You would be *diseased inside*. It was straight out of a David Lynch movie, hideous and inexplicable—the literal worm in the bud.[3]

Frankly, my girlfriend's job gave me the screaming meemies. I couldn't believe how casually she referred to her "clients," knowing what she did with them. I have a hard time looking people in the eye when meeting them, and I can barely bring myself to shake hands. But here my girlfriend was shoving a tube into their guts and politely removing their impacted shit! Sure, I danced for assholes—but she actually *washed* them. I was squeamish about hand-to-hand contact, but she was gloving up and swabbing out people's rectums. It was unthinkable.

So of course I became obsessed. I pestered my poor girlfriend for professional details unmercifully.

If she didn't give me enough detail in an attempt to preserve the privacy and dignity of her clients, I'd angrily demand painstaking specifics. *How long was the tapeworm? Was it still alive? Was it wiggling on the way out?* She'd roll her eyes and sigh, but like the health professional she was, she always answered my questions matter-of-factly—simply, but with an instructorly eye toward practical detail. I imagined her bedside manner to be soothing and brisk: pretty much exactly what you'd want from a

---

3. Bring on the dancing midgets!

93

HOST

stranger to whom you're entrusting the care and comfort of your ass. I tried not to giggle when she said things like "fecal mass" and "rectal straining."

The main part of the job was irrigating her customers' colons, but the *other* part of the job—my girlfriend patiently informed me during one of my SS-style interrogation sessions—was explaining what dietary issues were evident from the shit rinsed away during the irrigation process. In other words, my girlfriend looked at her clients' shit and *interpreted* it for them, like Rorschach blotches or chicken innards. She was like a wine steward—except instead of describing the bouquet, weight, and color of a particular vintage, she discerned telling gradations in the quality and mass of her customers' impacted waste, teasing out meaning from varying shades and certain textural subtleties.

This drove me wild. "You mean you're sitting there *as they're shitting*—I mean, getting *rinsed*—and you're talking about the actual shit with them? Like, you're pointing out specific details *as the shit comes out of their bodies?*" I admit I was out of control. But curiosity was like a fever, and the small portions of information allotted to me by my long-suffering girlfriend only inflamed my desire to know more about people with enough money to subcontract their own rectal hygiene.

"Okay, look," my girlfriend finally said. "Here's what happens. The client undresses and lies on his or her side. I come in and discuss their concerns about their session and answer any questions they may have at that point."

My cheeks felt hot. *"Like?"* I demanded.

My girlfriend held up her hand. "Just standard stuff! Like if they're curious about the procedure, or if it's their first time and

FLESH

they're nervous!" She glared at me. "You know, this is my *job*. I take it seriously, even if you don't. I *help* people, you know?"

"Yes! Yes! I know! Please, *please*, go on!"

I was transfixed—ravenous for the information she was doling out with infuriating slowness. At the same time, I knew that pressuring her too much would break the bank and I'd go home busted. Some slot machines you shake hard, and others you barely even jostle. My girlfriend was a jostler—if I harassed her too much, she'd lock. I had to let her relay information at her own pace with only the gentlest of nudges. I took a deep breath, held it, and released it in an audible *whoosh*.

"I know you help people, baby," I said. I reminded myself not to say *shit* again—it was *fecal material*. I'd known better. I'd just gotten excited.

"All right." She waited an excruciating eternity—*Get to the parasites! For the love of God, get to the worms!*—then sighed heavily. "You're such a toddler. What's next—finger-painting with your own doody?"

"Maybe," I said. "No! I mean, I'm just really interested in your work, honey." I held my breath. "Sweetheart? Your work? It's important, and stuff?"

"Well, it *is* important," she said. "A lot of people walk around with *five to ten pounds* of impacted feces clogging up their intestines! Not to mention, a lot of people—even nice, clean people with good eating habits—have parasites! They feel tired and run-down all the time, and they don't know why, but it's *shit* and *bugs* in their bodies, stealing their energy and making them feel bloated, constipated, and ill."

I bit my lip. "That sounds really . . . um . . . " *Sick. Revolting.*

Filthy. " . . . unbalanced. Like, um, metabolically." I had no idea what I was talking about, but *metabolically unbalanced* had to be better than any of the other words that came to mind.

My girlfriend warmed to her subject. "Okay, so we talk and I answer any questions they have. Then I gently insert a tube inside them that delivers body-temperature water slowly, until their lower intestine is filled. Then I reverse the flow and the water—and waste—drains out into a large machine with a glass panel on the front, so I can monitor the waste coming out. Then I do that a bunch more times until the waste water is mostly clear." She glared at me. *"Okay?"*

I nodded. I tried ESP. *Tapeworms!* I mentally commanded.

"If they have any parasites, I can see them as the waste drains away. The tube is clear and so is the glass panel on the irrigation machine, so I can observe what's being shed."

Jackpot.

"Do you tell them?" I croaked. "If they have them?"

"Of course I do," she replied tartly. "Why else would I be looking at their feces? For fun? They need to know what's in their own bodies and how to be more healthful!" She looked at me and spoke with an air of grave authority. "For a lot of people, it's really healing."

She was touchy, but my girlfriend's disinclination to talk about her professional life was understandable. Nobody wants to be treated as a curiosity, not even people who spend forty hours a week power-washing shit out of other people's assholes. After all, I was working as an adult entertainer—I knew all about being treated like a specimen by people seeking titillating first-person work stories. I had to tread carefully.

Three sevens, baby. Come on.

"What's the grossest thing you've ever seen drain out of someone's—" I was going to say *ass. No! No! Caution!* "—um, body?"

My girlfriend answered wearily. "An entire floret of broccoli," she said.

I was a little let down. "A broccoli?" I repeated.

"Yeah, an entire floret. A big one. It was just wedged in there, undigested and whole."

"Oh . . . " I had to admit I had been expecting something more sinister—maybe a condom, or something made of metal. A broccoli floret wasn't that gross—it wasn't even that surprising. I was disappointed.

"But the thing was, I asked the client when he last ate broccoli. And he said he hated it and didn't eat it often. The last time he'd had it was a year ago, at a friend's wedding. It had just been sitting in there since then, rotting and causing cramping and gas."

"Dude, he had a year-old *broccoli* up in there?" I gasped.

"Yeah," she said. "Oh, and he had tapeworms, too. Big flat ones. One was wrapped around the floret, actually. It was alive. It was convulsing, flexing, and whipping around—almost as if it knew it was being dislodged and was mad about it."

She paused, choosing her words with care. "I'm guessing it was probably several feet long. The broccoli-and-worm mass almost didn't fit through the tube—I was worried I'd have to extract it manually somehow. I wasn't sure what to do. But eventually part of the worm broke off, then the rest of the mass fit through. Both parts were still alive though—those worms are really hardy! You can see how they'd survive in someone's intestines really well, just breaking apart and multiplying and growing bigger and longer, the longer you have them." She shrugged. "I mean, if you don't get them out."

I felt hot and dizzy. The payoff had been worth it, all right, but now that I was considering the image of a broccoli floret wrapped in a living, flexing tapeworm like a scallop in a strip of bacon, I wondered if I was going to faint. How did my girlfriend ever eat her lunch four hours into her shift, knowing that after her meal she'd be coming back to another series of shit- and worm-plugged intestines? How did she ever eat *anything?*

My girlfriend looked at me sharply. "That's where *I* come in, you know. It's a really necessary service we provide."

I forced myself to stop thinking about parasite-laden shit. I had to. If I didn't, I knew I'd faint and my girlfriend would feel used. I'd reached the pinnacle of grossness for the day—rotten, worm-infested broccoli—which, if you thought about it, was pretty foul after all. Broccoli had never been my favorite vegetable anyway. I wondered how I'd feel the next time I saw it in my girlfriend's stir-fry. I imagined staring down at my plate at the wok-tossed floret—then pictured it wrapped in a long strip of onion.

I kissed my girlfriend on the mouth. "I love you so much, baby," I said tenderly.

I really did. She gave me a lot to think about. Also, my asshole was feeling really itchy, and I wanted to slip into the bathroom to wipe compulsively. I regularly used up all her double-quilted girly toilet paper and replaced it with big industrial rolls of Scott, which I stole from work. She never complained, but every time I came over to her apartment the Scott was gone and there was another roll of delectably soft Charmin next to her spotless commode. It seemed to me that because of her work, my girlfriend

FLESH

paid attention to assholes and thoughtfully gave them the things they liked—her affection for me was proof enough of that. She was conscientious about both set and setting, from making sure her bathroom was a clean and pleasant place to poop to supplying the expensive paper I coveted but never bought for myself. She really knew how to live, and I loved her for that.

And a few days later when I woke up in the middle of the night, screaming and clawing at an invisible flatworm grown horribly large, determined to bore through my skin and into my guts in search of a broccoli floret to call its own, she just held me tight, bless her sweet and healing heart.

FAT

TODAY I'M SLOW-BAKING A VANILLA CUSTARD TO GOLDEN, nutmeg-crusted perfection in a 300-degree oven. I have Indian butter chicken percolating in my Crock-Pot, making my whole apartment smell of curry and spice and tomatoes and yes, *butter*—five wonderful, flavorful tablespoons of organic salted— and when it's done I'm going to fork-shred the chicken and ladle it over hot jasmine rice and serve the whole glorious spicy mess with a dollop of cool, sweet mango chutney.

I'm not having guests over, either. No—I'm cooking all this lovely food for myself, and I'm going to eat as much of it as I want, sitting with a good book and a tall, cool glass of beer. I'm hungry, and I look forward to eating my supper. I can smell the hot butter, and it's maddening, so ambrosial I want to yank off the lid of my slow-cooker and plunge my spoon into it and devour every bit of sauce right now. It smells so good I want to roll in it. I'm undone—a slavering pet frisking around my own kitchen, begging for treats.

Fat makes food taste really, really good.

It keeps your hair glossy and your curves plump and most of all, it gives a certain silky roll to each mouthful, a smooth satin glide across your palate that feels like a long, deep kiss. Fat is flavor, from elegant infused olive oil to the down-home raunch of poured-off Jimmy Dean sausage grease. Fat is where flavor *lives*. Fat is the good part. Fat wraps around fiber and eases its passage, makes it palatable, dresses it up. Fat is like a good, expensive pair of black boots: It goes with anything, always adds welcome flair, and gives you a sexy, ass-swaying strut.

Eschewing fat in the name of health is a losing proposition. When you deny yourself fat, you recalibrate your sense of satiety. *More*, your body demands. So, meaning well, you give it more fatless food. Quantity, however, does not replace quality. Your body knows the difference. It wants a certain amount of deliciousness, and whether you get that deliciousness from one lovely, crisp piece of buttered toast or from thirty dry, mealy, cardboard-flavored fat-free crackers, your body will eat until it is satisfied. As a result, we tend to take in far more calories when we restrict our fat consumption.

I know from fat. I used to *be* fat. I was fat, and I didn't want to be, so I bought a lot of fat-free products, from salad dressings to those horrible stale-tasting cookies in the green boxes, each fat-free treat as packed with sugar and calories as three normal cookies. I also starved myself. But I was hungry all the time. I would have an apple and a container of fat-free yogurt for breakfast, I'd skip lunch, and I'd have a can of fat-free soup and one abstemious slice of dry bread for dinner. To my horror, no matter how little I ate (or how terrible my food tasted), I stayed fat. I even got fatter. I was beside myself—I couldn't believe what was happening. I exercised. I weighed myself. I baked potatoes in the microwave, broke them open, and ate the waxy, semicooked chunks of potato flesh with lemon juice and black pepper (150 calories). I bought low-calorie fat-free bread (50 calories per slice). I ate can after can of dry, water-packed tuna. I drank Crystal Light. Nothing I ate gave me any pleasure whatsoever—most of it tasted like paper, and the items that didn't taste like paper tasted like chemicals. *Why was I still fat?*

Finally, I gave up. I moved to New York and I started eating whatever I wanted. Fuck it—I was already fat; what could it hurt? All of a sudden there were worlds of food to explore, and I didn't want to miss a thing. I wanted to mouth New York City like a baby, tasting every neighborhood, every cuisine, every nook and cranny of the big, dirty city I loved. I wanted to lick the pavement, suck on subway tokens like hard candy, guzzle water from fountains, take the city inside me like a lover. I wanted it to change me from the inside out.

I bought hot dogs from carts with plenty of mustard and onions and shredded sauerkraut ladled up from greasy luke-warm tanks of water. I bought giant flappy triangles of pizza that dripped hot oil down my forearms, staining my sleeves. I bought cartons of good Greek coffee in the blue-and-white key-patterned cups. I learned to order it "regular," meaning loaded with cream. A giant muffin to go with my coffee only cost a dollar, and they were baked fresh all day. I liked the ones with chocolate chips. I also liked the black-and-white cookies available in any deli. They were half-vanilla and half-chocolate, Frisbee-size. I ate my black-and-white cookies with two hands, gnawing equal portions of each side in turn so as not to run out of one flavor too soon.

In my Brooklyn neighborhood there was more pizza—better than I'd ever had before in my life, from real Italian pizzerias. There were Chinese dumplings, too, pork and vegetarian, dipped in soy sauce mixed with "duck sauce," which was a sweet orange jelly squeezed out of a plastic sleeve. There were crumbly rice balls that tasted of salt and meat grease, as big as baseballs. There were pounds of Italian shortbread cookies, some dipped in frosting and sprinkles, and some plain. They came in big pink bakery boxes tied up with real string.

I went to kosher dairy restaurants, making sure to dress modestly to show my respect to the local Hasidim, who drank their coffee with fruit jam instead of sugar. I learned to order big crusty slabs of rice pudding as dense and solid as cake, along with strudels and kugel and *rugelach* and other guttural, delicious fruit-filled pastries. I ate vinegary knishes and little dumplings stuffed with cabbage. In the delis that served meat, I ordered sandwiches so thick I had to press the slices of rye bread together, savagely compressing piled mounds of corned beef and pastrami into pink and purple slabs in order to take a bite. I gnawed on oversize bagels the size of catcher's mitts. My front teeth were constantly coated in bright yellow deli mustard. I washed everything down with Dr. Brown's Cel-Ray soda, I no longer gave a flying fuck about being fat. There were plenty of fat people in New York—I was merely one of many. We ran to catch our morning express trains clutching Greek coffees and crullers just like everyone else. New York's famous indifference meant I could eat when I was hungry and stop when I was full without feeling scrutinized or even noticed. In a city of so many people, nobody gave a damn about one chubby Seattleite gobbling pizza from a sheet of greasy wax paper.

And I started getting thinner.

All that fat—all that *flavor*—and my body could finally relax and stop hoarding miserly calories, tricked by my own willpower into believing I was starving to death. My skin bloomed, and the extra weight I was carrying fell away, and at first I just thought my pants were getting "stretched out" because they were old and losing elasticity. Soon it became clear that my fat-enhanced diet was responsible for my loss of what was eventually six dress sizes.

You'd think this would have changed my life. Most people are conditioned by a lifetime of Before and After pictures—showing first, a lumpen, ashy mound of a woman and, second, a maple-brown fitness model posing in a thong—to believe that massive weight loss results in a better, happier, sexier life. But in reality, it only meant that none of the clothes I wore before I moved fit anymore—and that the Italian men in my neighborhood stopped making kissing noises as I walked by with my new, sleeker build. I bought two new pairs of pants and three new shirts. I didn't buy anything else to wear because I was still spending most of my money on food. I was pleased by my shrinking girth, but I didn't feel like I owned it. I kept waiting to balloon up again once my body finally figured out how much food I was actually consuming. I felt like I was getting

FLESH

away with something but feared getting caught and punished. I was sure that after six months of unbridled eating, I'd wake up resembling the six-hundred-pound man who had to be airlifted through his own ceiling for medical intervention.

Eventually my size stabilized. I had become a perfectly reasonable size 12—morbidly obese to the fashion industry, it's true, but medium-size to the rest of the world. I remembered being fat and miserable in Seattle, feeling hungry—no, *starved*, my hunger lighting up every moment of every day like a flashing neon DAN-GER sign—and I found I vastly preferred the alternative: eating freely and joyfully in a city I loved. They say you are what you eat, and that if you feast on fat you'll *become* fat—but the diet industry's economic interest lies in keeping us fat through misinformation so they can sell us more weight-loss products, and I never wanted to eat another cardboard-flavored confection in my life. Gnawing on a black-and-white cookie in a deli in lower Manhattan, I realized the diet experts had been lying all along.

So now I eschew anything labeled "diet" or "lite," and I eat when I'm hungry, and I try to make sure that everything I devour is as delicious and whole as it can be. And I've worn the same dress size for more than twelve years.

Who says diets don't work? Of course they do. The ones that involve deprivation, hunger, obsession, displeasure, and calorie-counting will result in inexorable weight gain, self-loathing, and depression, just as they're designed to do. But the diets dictated by our own appetites—the ones that nourish us with flavor, fat, and deliciousness—will result in us being the size we're meant to be, whether that's 2 or 12 or 20.

Ladies, call off the hunger strike. Real women eat fat.

RED GRAVY

SPAGHETTI SAUCE IS THE RORSCHACH TEST OF THE CULINARY world: What's telling in the details of any recipe isn't about which ingredients are included and which are left out; it's about what each individual cook thinks *should* be in it, and *shouldn't*.

Nearly everyone who prepares food, amateur or professional, believes their spaghetti sauce to be the best—whether they spend all day dicing organic hothouse tomatoes, mincing fresh basil from their own herb gardens, and crushing garlic with an imported European press; or whether they open a can of Ragú, toss in some garlic salt, and call it their own special recipe.

But similar to the explanations created to justify the appearance of nonrepresentational inkblots, the personality-revealing aspects of spaghetti sauce live in the details of the story any cook tells about his or her perfect sauce. I've noticed a frequent moral cast to each narrative straddling related senses of rightness and righteousness: Every cook seems to believe that a successful sauce must be prepared *one* particular way, and *only* that way—*their* way, of course. Passions run hot. Two cooks in the same kitchen can end up sparring like ferrets over a single spoonful of white sugar if one chef was raised to believe that adding granulated sweetener to spaghetti sauce brings out a certain mellow, sun-kissed, tomato-y tang, and the other scorns its addition as a disgraceful and inauthentic Chef Boyardee–ism.

But I'm less interested in some kind of pure ideal of spaghetti sauce—an Ultimate Spaghetti Sauce recipe culled from thousands of recipes passed down for generations and countless handwritten notations in the margins of store-bought cookbooks. No, I'm more interested in what *you* put in *your* sauce. Because I don't think any kind of objectivity is possible. I think spaghetti sauce is something unique, like fingerprints. I think my sauce is mine and yours is yours, and, furthermore, I have a Fancy Spaghetti Sauce that I make for guests I'd like to seduce and a Modest Spaghetti Sauce that I make for myself at the end of the month, when I'm broke and hungry. You may have a couple of different sauces, too. I'd like to eat them—especially at the end of the month—instead of my own Modest Sauce, a sad mélange of canned tomato sauce, oregano, and old, soft onions. (Maybe I should try adding a spoonful of sugar.)

THE KEY TO my Fancy Spaghetti Sauce is sausage, honestly. Lots of sausage. And lots of *different* sausage, if you want to be decadent. Lamb, veal, pork, beef—even chicken or turkey. If it's ground and spiced, throw it in! The more animals simmering in harmony on your range the better! In a stew of garlicky tomato sauce, creatures locked in perpetual combat in Nature can relax and enjoy each other's company, putting their differences aside in pursuit of a common goal: deliciousness.

If you're a vegetarian, I'm sorry, but you're missing out. Sausage—real meat sausage, not the vegan kind made from sawdust, cornmeal, and animal-byproduct-free glue—is almost indescribably savory. You can dine alone on inexpensive supermarket sausage braised in a single skillet with sauerkraut and new potatoes, or you can dress up boutique meat-counter sausage with fresh herbs and breadcrumbs on a bed of field greens for guests, because sausage is as confident and charming as a bunch of offal stuffed into intestinal casing can be. Sausage says, *I'm glad you came*, and *Don't you look beautiful tonight*. Sausage is both regal and wonderfully proletarian. Sausage is down-to-earth, unpretentious—comfortable grilled and served with only a dab of stone-ground mustard or dressed in a velvety blanket of gravy over peppered grits and eggs. Sausage is a special friend to poor people in particular—our patron saint of chopped fat and spice and connective tissue and scrap meat—because it lends a large amount of flavor to cheap and filling foods like rice and noodles and potatoes. Sausage is *good*. Sausage *does* good. I love sausage!

You could make this recipe without sausage, if you wanted to make some kind of point about Not Needing Meat, Thank You Very Much—I Get Enough Protein From Combining Starches, And Besides, The Planet Can't Afford It. But remember: Sausage will always take you back. Sausage has a lot of love to give. You just have to whisper *Yes* to it and sausage will sweep you away to

FLESH

gustatory paradise, I promise, no matter how many starches you combined for your joyless little lunch or how earnestly you tell yourself that meat-free soy patties are "better than the real thing." Ha! Sure—like a punch in the face from a surly political vegan is better than getting tongue-kissed by your own sweet lover!

ANYHOW—TO MAKE my Fancy Sauce, start by chopping onions.

Actually, wait. This is my Fancy Sauce, so start by pouring yourself a glass of red wine. Any red will do. You're gonna cook with half of it, so don't spend too much, because it really doesn't matter. You know Gato Negro—the red wine that used to be packaged with *an actual tiny black plastic cat* dangling from a string around the neck of each bottle?

I bought a bottle of Gato Negro about six months ago for old times' sake, and I'm not gonna lie to you: To my thirty-six-year-old palate, it really sucked. I found it excruciatingly tannic, as if every sip actually robbed moisture from my mouth instead of adding to it, like cotton batting stuffed into a wound—and the worst part was, *there was no plastic cat!* There was just a *picture* of a black cat on the label!

But my point is simply this: Even Gato Negro will do. It'll do to drink—and at about $5 a bottle (last time I checked), it won't break your bank. It cooks up wonderfully well, and despite its undeniably astringent mouth-feel, it'll get you loosey goosey enough to prepare my Fancy Sauce with a little verve and, dare I say it, *panache*. Because, and I didn't mention this earlier, but boy is Fancy Sauce fun to make! And it's so damn good! And it will get you laid! I'm telling you, you'll want to have wine.

Which will mean getting at least one decent bottle. Maybe two if you're showing off by cooking in front of your guest—a move I highly recommend. Everyone likes to feel pampered, and what's more pampering than cooking a meal for someone? You'll also appear competent, grown-up, and together—like you're enough of an adult to keep actual ingredients in your kitchen instead of just plastic jugs of bottom-shelf liquor, half-empty jars of rancid cocktail garnishes, and boxes of Girl Scout cookies and Honey Smacks. When I'm looking to get laid, I at least like to pretend an interest in my own nutritional welfare.

Okay, so pour that glass of red wine. Take a sip. If you're entertaining, make sure your guest's glass is full (and *stays* full).

Now, get out your cutting board—wooden or plastic, it doesn't matter. Chop up one whole onion. While you're at it, chop up a green pepper or two. Don't worry about cutting perfect little cubes. If you're OCD by nature, you really need to harness your urge toward chop overkill, because, honestly, bigger pieces of onion and pepper will cook down and get soft and will ultimately make your Sauce more visually interesting. You don't want the Fancy Sauce to look like it came from a jar. The whole point is, *it doesn't.* So leave chunks.

Okay. Now it's time to get out your sausage. If you bought loose sausage meat (the kind that looks like ground beef, often sold as "Italian sausage" or "sweet sausage"), just take it out of the fridge and unwrap it. If you bought link sausage ("breakfast" sausage, andouille, hot links, kielbasa—basically anything that's hot dog– or cigar-shaped and in a casing), slice each link into pieces diagonally, so you get little extended disc shapes. Or cut your sausage up how- ever you like. (*I* like the extended disc shapes, but then again, I drink $5 red wine, so maybe you have your own idea of what you want and that's totally okay . . . you big snob!)

Now get out a big skillet. Cast iron is best. But whatever. Make it a big one. You want your ingredients to have plenty of room to move.

Put the skillet on your range, turn the heat up to medium-ish, and let it get hot. (A good test for skillet heat: Take a finger-ful of water and flick it at the pan. If the water hisses and hops around, congratulations! Your skillet is officially hot enough for the next part of this recipe! But if the water droplets you flick just sit there, turn the heat up a bit or wait a little longer, because your pan isn't ready yet.)

Once your pan is hot, throw in some olive oil—just a sprin-kle or two, fast fast. You're not trying to cover the whole bottom of the skillet with oil, but you do want to have enough so that your ingredients won't stick until the fat in the sausage melts and takes over. If you don't have olive oil, you can use any fat you've got around the house—lard, Crisco, canola, anything. Don't use butter, though. If you want extrasuper bonus Fancy Sauce points, use bacon grease that you've saved in a crock in your fridge since the last time you fried up a pan of bacon.

(I am taking a conscious aside here. Bacon is truly the Wonder Food. Nearly every assemblage of ingredients it touch-es becomes infinitely better—more flavorful, more savory, more complex, more *layered* in taste and deliciousness. When you fry bacon, pour off the grease and save it. Bacon grease is liquid gold! When you cook with bacon grease, people will love whatever you make for them and will clamor for more, and they'll never know it's because you're using culinary voodoo. It's almost unfair. But again, if you're looking to get laid, you gotta pull out the big guns. Sugar in the sauce is nothing—when I haven't gotten any play in months, I seriously consider adding Rohypnol.)

Dump the onions, green peppers, and sausage into the hot skillet with the oil (or bacon grease) and use a wooden spoon to keep everything moving around so the food doesn't stick to the bottom of the pan. If your sausage is loose, use the wooden spoon to separate the lump of sausage into individual-size chunks. Just kind of stir everything together, allowing the sausage to brown and the veggies to get nice and soft and coated with olive oil and the meat-grease that will ooze out of the sausage. Turn the heat down a little bit if it seems like anything's getting too brown too fast, or if the pan starts smoking. Keep stirring. If you're using link sausages cut up into discs, be sure to flip the discs over with your spoon so both sides of each sausage-coin get browned.

Now everything's gonna go fast, so pay attention. You may want to take this opportunity to pour yourself more wine. Top off your guest's glass while you're at it, you Continental seducer.

Get out a big stockpot. It should have a lid, but if you don't have one, you can always cover it with tinfoil. Once the sausage is mostly brown, scrape the onion/green pepper/sausage mixture into the stockpot. And listen, the sausage should only be *mostly* brown—some pink is actually good, because it's gonna cook all the way in the sauce and you definitely don't want the meat to be cooked into dry, hard little mouse turds. Don't overcontrol the Sauce! Trust the Sauce! It knows what it's doing—it just wants you to be relaxed with it and to add everything in, but then it really just wants to be left alone as it transforms from an assemblage of ingredients into vibrant,

FLESH

cohesive Sauce. Be a Jedi Master about this. If you're finding yourself uptight, simply have more wine.

Speaking of wine, pour a little into the skillet, and use the wooden spoon to scrape up as many of the browned and crusty bits sticking to the bottom of the pan as you can. (This is called *deglazing*, if you want to be all fancy about it.) Dump the wine/crusty bits mixture into the stockpot over the onions, green peppers, and sausage.

Now: Throw in a few cans of tomato sauce. If you have any cans of diced or crushed tomatoes, throw those in too. You can throw in one of those minicans of tomato paste if you like, but don't add more than one can of paste or your sauce will get too thick. Stir everything around with your wooden spoon. Fancy Sauce freezes beautifully and keeps for months, so you may want to make a whole bunch of it, if you can. It pretty much just depends on how many cans of tomato products you have in your kitchen, and on the capacity of your stockpot.

The fun part of Fancy Sauce starts now. Gather up any or all of the following things: oregano, rosemary, thyme, parsley, fennel, garlic powder, minced garlic (I use the fresh minced garlic in water or oil sold in jars near the bins of dry garlic bulbs in nearly any medium-to-large supermarket—I go through vast quantities of this, and yeah, I know it's not as good as mincing your own garlic but I just throw in a few extra spoonfuls and call it good), Lawry's Seasoned Salt (if you like it—otherwise regular salt), black pepper, cayenne pepper, white pepper, poultry seasoning, Italian seasoning, dill (not too much of this), and basil.

All the herbs and spices I refer to above should be *dried*, not fresh, but if you have a bunch of fresh herbs lying around, throw 'em in—why not? Throw all the herbs/spices/seasonings you've picked out from the list above into your stockpot, which should be on your range on the lowest heat setting. Use *lots* of oregano, garlic, and pepper—like big bountiful handfuls! Use small amounts of fennel and dill—like modest palmfuls. Everything else, just go medium. But if you're using garlic salt instead of garlic *powder*, be cautious with the amount you use because it's mostly just salt, and you don't want your Fancy Sauce to taste like the Dead Sea. Dump in a few glasses of wine for good measure.

Let your Sauce simmer on the range uncovered, on the lowest possible heat setting, for three or four hours. Stir it every now and again. After a while taste it—it may need more spices or more salt. Correct the seasoning. Once it's cooked down to a nice thick saucy consistency, cover the pot with the lid (or tinfoil) to keep any more liquid from evaporating. Mostly, *leave it alone*—a good sauce doesn't need much prodding. (Alternatively, put your Sauce into a Crockpot on the lowest possible setting, cover it, and forget about it overnight—no stirring needed.)

Once your Sauce has cooked down to the right consistency and you've covered the pot to keep it from reducing any further, you can serve it anytime. Leaving it on the burner just develops the flavor, which is nice if it's cold out and you want to keep your kitchen warm and fragrant, or if you're waiting for guests to arrive. Sometimes at this point I'll throw in a few packages of frozen chopped spinach and possibly a can of drained marinated artichoke hearts, but this is totally up to you—I just like a lot of *stuff* in my sauce, and sneaking in veggies is also a great way to add nutrients. (Be sure to allow the sauce to heat the frozen stuff through before you serve it.)

FLESH

If you aren't planning on eating your thickened sauce immediately, remove it from the range and refrigerate it.

Serve your Sauce over pasta with crusty French bread torn into chunks by hand. (Cutting French bread just squashes it and looks overcontrolling, whereas tearing it up gives you a devilish air of spontaneity. Don't be the culinary equivalent of the person at the party who can't stop chopping up blow.) Serve with candles on the table and another bottle of wine.

Your kisses will taste like garlic, but if your guest isn't a vampire, it won't matter. Besides, if you've been following my directions carefully, you're both probably pretty toasted. Skip dessert and go directly to bed. Congratulations, you hot-booty gourmand! You're getting laid!

(The last time I made Fancy Sauce for a guest, I noticed his come tasted like fresh garlic the next morning. It was like comefredo sauce! I felt like I was having sex in an Olive Garden! This may not be to your preference, so be warned, and take the shot on your tits accordingly if you're not into the prospect of garlic-flavored man-butter the morning after your Fancy Sauce dinner date. I can only assume that my cooch tasted of garlic similarly, but I did not choose to *deglaze my own pan* that morning so that knowledge is, unfortunately, lost to history.)

FORBIDDEN FRUIT

THINGS I'VE EATEN THAT MOST PEOPLE PROBABLY HAVEN'T:

I.

I was supping with a friend in a restaurant in downtown Seattle. His fiancée was a staunch vegetarian, so when he and I went out to eat we always picked restaurants that featured meat and more meat. She knew about our *affaire de viande* and indulged him in his occasional bacchanal, as long as he brushed his teeth vigorously afterward and didn't come home with animal leftovers. I was his partner in crime for all meat-related offenses, a temptress of beef and pork. When we went out it was always Carnival. We ate flesh like robber barons, picking our teeth and groaning.

Steak was old hat, so we'd met at an upscale Brazilian restaurant famous for a particular dish few other local restaurants had the guts to offer. Its menu called the dish "grilled sweetbreads," which I knew were offal—but what kind? Could Brazilian sweetbreads be similar to Mexican *tripa* or Scottish haggis?

I was pretty sure I didn't want to eat another animal's intestines. A living creature's intestines are, essentially, sausage casings full of shit—and no matter how much you soak and rinse them after butchering the beast, the rubbery membranes are still haunted by the Ghost of Shits Past.

I wasn't even into analingus with my own species. I mean, I was willing to get my own asshole licked when I had to in pursuit of a good lay, but I wasn't about to pay $20 for the privilege of ingesting a portion of cow GI tract, "grilled" or not.

I read on. The menu text describing the plate specified that the innards in question were, in fact, a calf's pancreas gland.

Well, that was completely different!

In humans, the pancreas is a long organ that wraps around the stomach and secretes both digestive enzymes and glucose-regulating hormones. The word *pancreas* comes from the Greek words for "all flesh" or "all meat," reflecting the pancreas's uniquely spongy, cutletlike composition. Furthermore, the pancreas is high up enough in the gastrointestinal system that it doesn't have anything to do with shit. It's just an innocent organ, pumping out chemicals. The enzymes and hormones it secretes are *pre*shit.

I had to try some. I figured that something called "all meat" must be at least a little bit delicious.

When the Brazilian waiter came I ordered the sweetbreads.

"You are sure?" he asked. "It is, you know—" he gestured vaguely at his stomach.

"Yes," I said. "It's *pancreas*."

The waiter looked doubtful. "Yes?"

I smiled. "It's part of the *digestive system*. But it's not directly involved with the production of actual—"

My friend kicked my ankle under the table.

I closed my mouth and folded my hands. "That's all," I said. "Thank you."

Our waiter shrugged, retrieved our menus, and disappeared.

Eventually, our food showed up—delivered by the busboy.

"Thank you!" I said. "I'm really looking forward to trying this." I pointed at my plate, heaped with rice and grilled meat.

"No English," he said determinedly. He deposited a full basket of bread on our table and fled.

Without further ado, I dug into my pile of cow innards.

Grilled pancreas tastes like bacon but has a tender, melt-away texture not unlike its fellow internal organ, liver.[1] Eating grilled pancreas is a lot like eating bacon-flavored scrambled eggs: The texture is so delicate it tends to fall apart when you try to use a fork. After a few mishaps, I learned to heap my pancreas onto pieces of bread and gobble it as an open-faced sandwich.

"Dude, check it out," I giggled, my mouth full of bread and grilled pancreas. "It's a *glandwich*." I laughed until I choked, spat out the offending bit of bread, then popped it back in my mouth. It was too good to waste on dainty manners.

The bacon taste was so pronounced it was almost too concentrated, but the bread helped disperse the intensity of the flavor. As I devoured my pancreas, I felt exhilarated and gleeful. I was the Hannibal Lecter of the cow world!

I cleaned my plate and wished for more, mopping the pancreas juice up with the last piece of bread in the basket. The Greeks were right: Pancreas *was* all meat! It was so meaty it was like meat boiled down to its essentiality—pure meat-taste with all of the filler lifted away. It was like the Platonic idea of meat. It was Meat.

I was full, my lips were slicked with grease, and my belly felt bisected by the waistband of my pants. I wondered if the additional digestive enzymes I'd just ingested would make the metabolization of my meal that much swifter.

"Do you think cow enzymes work the same as human enzymes?" I asked my friend eagerly. "Do you think my shit will be noticeably different in any way?"

My friend shrugged. His interest in Science seemed to wane periodically, but my own never flagged. I made a mental note to call him with the results of my inquiry the next day.

---

1. A liver aside: I once had a friend who worked as a counselor for a local AIDS organization. Her job was to interview folks who'd made appointments to be tested in order to help them assess the elements of their lifestyle that put them at risk of contracting HIV. As a result, she had to ask a whole slew of questions about her clients' personal sexual practices.

One of the questions she asked was, of course, "Do you engage in oral-anal contact?" As follow-up to a "yes" answer, one young man volunteered that not only did he lick ass enthusiastically, he also engaged in coprophagia—the practice of shit-eating. He wasn't ashamed of himself and related this information matter-of-factly, adding that he didn't eat *everyone's* shit—he avoided that kind of intimacy with casual bar pickups and tricks. He only ate the shit of people he really cared about.

Emboldened by his frankness, my friend asked him what shit tasted like.

"Liver," he responded without hesitation. "It tastes a lot like liver."

Which makes sense, the liver being a major player in excretory functioning. (The texture, he added, was similar to a coarsely milled country pâté.)

As a child, I dreaded the nights my dad would fry liver with onions, and I only ate it when I was forced to.

I'd always thought that liver tasted like shit.

Now it turns out that shit actually tastes like liver.

Mysteriously, our waiter never came back to our table. The busboy dropped our check.

I was more than satisfied with my meal. Sweetbreads: two thumbs up.

II.

I finally had a chance to try marrow at a fancy San Francisco restaurant during dinner with my editress and several other people from the company that publishes my books. It was listed as an appetizer, served "in the bone, with grilled bread." I'd been curious about marrow ever since I'd read about its use as a savory sauce for beef in *Larousse Gastronomique,* so I ordered it excitedly, promising to share bites with the rest of the table.

The marrow arrived as promised—shockingly—in a sawed-off segment of femur standing upright on my plate. The bone was like a thick stem surrounded by daisy petals of charred bread. My plate came furnished with a long-handled meat coke-spoon small enough to reach deep into the interior of the bone.

I felt almost dazed with the savagery of it, like a caveman about to feast after a successful hunt. There was no hiding the fact that I was about to devour roasted blood cells from the middle of a mighty, once-living creature's bone. I was the Antivegan, unapologetically carnivorous, a devout meat-eater staking my claim and taking my Communion. I wanted to gnaw the bone, to grind my teeth on it, to lick and suck it, howling under a full moon. I wanted to smear the blood across my face.

Instead, I used the tiny spoon to scrape the cooked blood out of the bone primly, then spread it on a delicate morsel of bread.

I'd imagined marrow to be coarse and grainy, almost like a

concentrated meat paste. Instead it was surprisingly gelatinous, with a slimy pull similar to the viscosity boiled okra lends to gumbo. My mouth wanted to reject it. It felt like someone else's spitty tongue in my mouth—a sour alien blob that was only remotely meat-flavored, as if the person with the interloping tongue had just eaten a hamburger. I didn't feel red-blooded and savage— I felt like I'd just popped out and swallowed my quarry's raw eyeball by mistake.

My editress tried a spoonful. "Oh, it's like meat-flavored snot," she said, wrinkling her nose.

I tried another bite. This time the marrow reminded me of a mouthful of come—a giant, oysterish, frothy load. I swallowed it like a trouper. I'd always been good at that, never having developed a particularly sensitive gag reflex. Who knew that I'd use that X-rated talent in the middle of a fancy San Francisco restaurant? In front of my editress, my publisher, and various others? I'd thought my days of public sexual performance were over, but apparently the focus had simply moved from my pussy to my esophagus.

The problem really was the texture. The flavor wasn't bad: It was subtly musky, oily, and animal-y, but not meaty like muscle fiber. It was more intimate than that. It was clear to me that I was eating a part of a cow that most people never ate, a part that could only be harvested through a great deal of effort. I'd eaten brains in a French restaurant once, and the taste of the marrow was similar: It was the taste of a body's secret spaces, the dignified parts not meant to nourish—the private areas reserved for the animal's own use. Somehow, eating the marrow seemed, well, not *wrong*, but certainly not right. I'd eaten brains, I'd eaten sweetbreads, but I'd never delved that deep inside a once-living creature's body before. I had gone, literally, to the bone of the matter.

As it cooled, the marrow began to smell like a wound, imperfectly cleaned. Was it actually *scabbing?* My stomach clenched lazily, like a greasy fist. I burped and tasted skeletal mass.

"How do you like it?" asked my editress. She'd sensibly ordered a beet salad, which looked delicious—cool and sweet in its lemony vinaigrette, like a pretty girl in a summer dress. "Is it what you'd thought it would be?"

"It tastes like an old, bloody tampon," I said. The table went silent. My publicist pushed her plate away.

"Sorry," I muttered.

I would not order marrow again, at least not by itself or as a spread for toast. But in all fairness, I would try it in a traditionally prepared French sauce over beef, because I think the heat and the texture of the sauce might fix the aspects of the marrow I found so distressing. As part of a sauce, I think it would be easier to ignore the marrow's grisly origins.

But I'm in no hurry to find out.

III.

Lord help me, I ate whale.

I know I'm going to hell for this. I know whales are endangered and that they're smart and beautiful behemoths of the deep. When I was little, my mom used to play a record of whale songs to lull me to sleep. So I know that what I did was wrong. I ate part of a gentle, singing giant.

A year ago, I was in a restaurant in Reykjavík, Iceland, with my date (another American). Raw whale was on the menu as an appetizer. I decided to order it.

"Americans don't like whale," said our waiter. "Perhaps the lamb?"

I took that as a challenge. I wanted whale! It was my right to order whale if I wanted to—it was right there on the menu! I imagined whale flesh as cool and pink, shell-colored and vaguely salty. All of a sudden I was starving for clean, delicious whale.

"I want whale," I said again. "Not lamb. I'm sure the lamb is good. But I want whale."

"I'll split it with you," my date said.

We stared at our waiter defiantly. We were Americans, sure, but we weren't *rubes*. We were from Seattle! He had no idea how much sushi we ate! The gauntlet had been thrown down. *Give us our whale!*

"Very good," he said, making a notation on his order pad. I felt a momentary pang of regret. I did love lamb—had I picked the right thing?

I could have lamb any day, though, I thought. I was in Iceland. It was time to eat whale.

When the whale arrived, it was a small chunk of shimmering gray tissue on a bed of greens. The smell of lye was very strong. I'd expected something similar to sashimi—fresh, raw whale—but it was clear from the aroma of the cube of whale muscle on the plate that Icelanders preserve whale the way Scandinavians make lutefisk, by soaking the raw, tender flesh in caustic soda. The smell was like two rude fingers poked up my nostrils. I hadn't known it would be like that—processed with what smelled like toilet cleaner.

My date looked ill, but game.

The waiter came back with two shots of schnapps. He explained that the kitchen had sent them to us gratis "to kill the taste." He stood back, assiduously wiping a clean table, in discreet observation of the crazy Americans who had ordered an expensive dish they would be too finicky to eat.

"You want to?" I said.

Despite the eye-watering chemical aroma, I was quietly exultant. Whale! It was so wrong—morally, legally, and environmentally wrong—in a tantalizing spectrum of malfeasance that made my mouth water. Nothing could stop me from eating it—not the smell, not its greasy, gray appearance, not the schnapps from the kitchen sent to intimidate, not the waiter standing by and waiting for us to turn up our pampered noses at something that would cost him half a day's pay. Not even a *Rainbow Warrior* full of Greenpeacers handing out flyers and trying to get our signatures on environmental petitions could stop me. I was in Iceland, and I was going to eat whale! I was a Viking—I came from the land of the ice and the snow!

I cut the chunk in half. The released lye fumes stung my eyes.

I glanced back at the kitchen. *I am your Overlord, bitches.*

"Okay, let's do it," I said.

After a brief pause, we both seized our forks and speared our halves of the whale-blob. I put my blob into my mouth before I could change my mind.

The lye opened my sinuses immediately but oddly, as it changed from a fragrance to a taste, it mellowed. My mouth didn't feel as if it were being cauterized by a household chemical the way I'd feared. Instead the lye turned gentle inside me, tasting sour and briny, almost like vinegar. It became *friendly.*

FLESH

I chewed rapidly, searching for the fish taste underneath the preservative. That couldn't be *it*, could it? Not just the taste of the lye—there had to be something else! Otherwise why the big deal and all the fuss? I poked my tongue into the mass of whale flesh desperately. *Oh, please—don't be a disappointment!*

And all of a sudden it blossomed in my mouth—WHALE! Like fish but bigger! Like raw steak but so much more vast! A land mammal's flesh tastes bloody and muddy from its earthy diet, and the seafood we catch with nets and traps tastes predictably fishy, but this was entirely from the deep sea and tasted like nothing I'd ever known before. It was like eating every swimming, crawling creature in the ocean, inhaling krill through gritted teeth. It was like eating the ocean itself.

Hammer of the gods.

The only way to explain the taste of whale is to multiply the taste and texture of raw shark exponentially, and if that definition's a shade too close to tautology, I have to shrug helplessly and give up. But I ate my chunk of whale, and as I swallowed it I knew that I would never taste anything that *big* ever again. I wanted to hold it in my mouth forever so I'd never forget it. Whale-meat was verboten in America and my trip to Reykjavík had cost thousands of dollars—the odds of me returning to Iceland for a second mouthful were slim. I felt miserable. To live without whale! To never taste this again!

I glanced at my date, who was already raising his glass of schnapps to his lips. So I raised mine in an ironic toast for our waiter's benefit, and drank. The anise taste of the liquor obliterated the whale as promised, and I was crestfallen. It was over. I couldn't bring it back.

"You *like* it?" Our waiter appeared by our table, an Icelandic genie summoned by the clink of our glasses against the table as we set them down. He smiled uncertainly, exposing uneven and yellowed teeth. *Like ivory,* I thought.

"I *really* liked it," I said.

All of a sudden my eyes filled with tears. *No more whale, ever again.*

"I really liked it," I said again. My date nodded, murmuring assent. Had he tasted the same thing I had? I had no idea how to ask. I'd just had a cosmic, LSD-like experience from eating an appetizer in a tiny Icelandic restaurant. If he'd experienced the same thing, there was no reason to slap inadequate words onto what had just happened. And if he hadn't, no amount of explanation would suffice.

Our fancy Reykjavík dinner continued. Afterward, we returned to the apartment we'd rented for the week, and I thought that the really terrible thing about eating something so important and singular and special is that once you've done it, you know that pretty much everything else you consume will be *lesser than.*

Some things the Devil tempts you to eat, laughing, the way he handed the apple of knowledge to poor Eve. Sometimes it's better not to know, so you can live in peaceful ignorance.

So eat and beware.

FLESH

Fried Chicken
Interlude:
Chickening Out

☠

I JUST MADE FOUR PIECES OF SOUTHERN FRIED CHICKEN.
I would have made more, but I only had four pieces of chicken,
so I shrugged and heated up a pan of Crisco and rolled those
four little pieces in batter and fried them till they were golden
brown and crispy and spicy and *dee*licious. Now my house smells
of frying grease, and I have two portions left over to eat "picnic-
style" tomorrow.

It's Saturday night and everyone's out doing whatever it is
people do on Saturday nights when they have money to blow on
entertainment.

Frankly, even if I had any buckage to spare, I wouldn't spend
it going out on Saturday night. All the amateur nightlife-loving
forty-hour-a-week office-job people are out, and they're usually

drunk and frenetic and trying to mate with each other, and that whole thing just makes me want to hide. Somewhere down the street, a man in Dockers is buying drinks for a twenty-two-year-old administrative assistant all dressed up in brand-new super-lowride bootcut jeans and kitten heels and a spaghetti-strapped tank top so nipple-delineating that wearing it would get any local lap dancer arrested for soliciting. But what's illegal in the privacy of an adult club is fine when worn on the street by a noncombatant, so Docker Man is getting an eyeful of tit for free, which is making him expansive with his credit card as he orders more liquor for his shivering, goose-pimpled date. It's cold out, but she's bravely soldiering on.

In addition to the major components of her Saturday night getup—the heels, the jeans, the sheer top—her accessories include carefully blown out highlighted hair, manicured nails, a store-bought tan, a tribal tattoo on her lower back, and—of course—her cell phone. Her going-out appearance took hours to refine, and that was just to get her presentable enough to get in the ring with all of the other expensively clad girls, her competitors. Four quickly gulped cosmos have girded her for engagement, but at her body weight, she's swaying in her heels.

She feels desired and beautiful and brave. Docker Man seems nice. She's not even that cold any longer, thanks to the heat of the liquor she drinks gratefully, when it is offered.

She's having fun, and she's a little drunky, and tomorrow when she wakes up in Docker Man's Eastside bed she'll snap her thong panties back on and try to tell herself that what she had the night before was exactly what she'd wanted. Fun. Sophisticated, girls'-night-out fun, culminating in a no-big-deal no-

FRIED CHICKEN INTERLUDE

strings-attached Saturday night hookup. It's all good—it doesn't have to mean anything! The *Sex and the City* girls pick up men all the time, and they're beautiful and rich and wear Prada and live in Manhattan!

Unfortunately, this is Seattle, and it's hard to afford Prada when you make administrative assistant wages. And in the light of day, Docker Man will look much older than she'd thought he was. There will be pictures of his kids on his bureau—both teenagers.

She'll flee his condo and use her cell phone to call for a cab. The ride back to the city will cost her $60, and the cabdriver will stare at her nipples through her tank top all the way home.

Which is fine, I suppose—she's old enough to make her own decisions. I spent my twenties getting fucked-up in clubs and going home with strangers myself, so it's not like I'm some kind of wise old owl with the perfect moral to a sordid tale, or whatever. I just don't want to watch it happen. That's all. I don't want to watch it. I've fucked my share of anonymous freaks, but I've never fucked any man with blow-dried hair and pleated business-casual khakis. I'm going to hang tight to that little bit of delusional superiority because tonight, all over Pioneer Square, hundreds of young women with professionally waxed vaginas are giving up the booty to hundreds of little office tin-pot dictators who are going to high-five their frat-brother friends in swinish congratulation on Monday morning. And the whole thing makes me completely unwilling to leave my house tonight, lest I inadvertently come across any Docker-wearing men in the company of tiny, sozzled, glitter-dusted office assistants and lose my mind contemplating the horrible predictability of the universe of Saturday night.

So I'm staying in tonight, trying to ignore the drunken

CHICKENING OUT

mating calls outside my apartment. All the squaring off and pairing off and *your place or mine*ing in the garb of freedom and excitement—oh, it makes me so tired. Casual sex is such a lie—there's nothing liberating about it; no warmth, no closeness—and frankly, the sex usually sucks. So tonight I'll bury my head under my pillows and pretend that all the kitten-heeled, manicured girls outside are turning down those last eagerly offered drinks and going home alone. It can't hurt to stay in and pretend.

That, and I have a brand-new library book. And store-bought brownie bites. I'm going to eat two (or possibly three) and then I'm going to brush my teeth and put on my comfy sleepin' panties and curl up for the night, to read my book in peace. After spending my twenties in the fray, I'm finally *hors de combat*. What sweet relief to have my bed to myself and know that my Sunday morning won't begin with a long cab ride home.

Tomorrow is picnic-style chicken, Grandma. Tonight your granddaughter is safe and sound—alone in her own apartment, sober as a judge.

FRIED CHICKEN INTERLUDE

III.
SWEET

INTRODUCTION

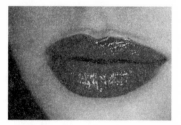

"I WANT YOU TO DRESS UP IN WHITE," SAID THE CUSTOMER. "All in white: white panties, white bra, white stockings. Do you have a white dress?"

Like a bride, I thought.

"Uh huh," I said. I'd already run his credit card through the machine, and now we were negotiating the specifics of the scene he was paying for. I did in fact have a white dress in my costume kit—it was a cheap and tatty satin slip that just barely covered my crotch. I wore it when I dressed up as a nurse, along with a little peaked cap perched at a fetching angle over my wig. The cap had an elastic chin strap, so it stayed on even when I was lying down or on all fours.

Nurse, bride, whatever. I didn't relish the idea of changing out of the black lingerie I was currently wearing. Why did they always want a complete wardrobe overhaul?

"White dress, white everything, got it," I said.

"One other thing," the customer said. He shifted his considerable weight nervously. He was a very large man, but then, a lot of them were. This one was younger than most—I guessed he was only twenty-five or twenty-six.

Why don't you have a girlfriend? I wondered wearily for the billionth time. It was hard to understand why men chose to pay a stranger to dress up in lingerie and watch them jerk off when most of them could have actual girlfriends whom they could actually fuck. This one was fat, sure, but he didn't smell bad—plenty of women would go out with him.

One other thing. Maybe it was going to be something disgusting, explaining his lack of nonpaid female companionship. "Sure, Chief," I said. "What might that be?"

"I, uh, want you to say something," he said.

Dirty talk—was that his big secret? I was disappointed.

"Like, tell you how much I want to fuck that big hard cock of yours?" I was on autopilot. I could dirty-talk all day without taxing a single brain cell. It was just the same words, over and over again, mixed around. "Or maybe tell you all about the way I like to play with my hot, wet pussy? No problem, Chief."

"N-no," the customer stammered. He took a deep breath.

"I want you to tell me you love me." He blushed. "You only have to do it once—when I'm, you know . . . "

Coming, I mentally finished his sentence for him. *You only have to do it once . . . when I'm coming.*

133

INTRODUCTION

And there it was: a wedding scene, complete with a bewigged bride and a tender defloration.

I'd made a career out of doing pretty much anything for money, but what he'd just asked me to do was outrageous. Love, in a place like this? I'd done a lot of filthy things, but selling out poor little *I love you* was not going to be one of them.

I thought of the word *profane*.

"No," I heard myself say. "I won't do that for you."

We stared at each other.

"I'll wear white, and I'll say anything else you want," I said. "But I'm not gonna say that. No way."

The customer grumbled, but he took the session with me anyway. He had to—he'd already paid for it. And I wore white, and screamed with pretend-orgasm while he dribbled into his own fist.

But neither of us said the word *love* to each other, as was only fitting in an ugly place where people go to mock everything *I love you* stands for.

WHEN I TELL this story at readings, middle-class, college-educated audiences tend to shift around and glance at each other, disappointed and disbelieving, suspicious that I'm somehow trying to make fools of them.

The working girls I read to, on the other hand, nod knowingly. I look down from the podium into their faces and I see that they're thinking of the words they could never be paid enough to say, too.

SWEET

LOVE IS THE one thing I've never lied about. *Will* never lie about. It's too important.

With all the monstrous things we do to each other in this world and all the ways we try to turn each other into objects for purchase, I truly believe that the most revolutionary thing we can do right now is to love each other, and to insist upon genuine human connection. Sweetness and sincerity are no longer luxuries—they're all we've got.

Well, that and the ability to shake our heads and laugh when the world gets too horrible to bear. If there's anything I learned from my years in the sex industry, it's that laughing is fighting back.

"SUGAR TOOTH" IS a bittersweet tale about a sweet girl.

"Pumpkin Pie" describes my scientific approach to getting laid, while "Treat" outs me as a size queen.

"Baby Ruth Man" is the tale of a torrid affair between a man and his favorite candy bar.

"Agapae" and "Trick" are war stories.

THIS CHAPTER'S FOR the dirty-sweet ones: the hos, the queers, the artists, the circus freaks, the poets, the drunks, the hurt ones, the angry ones, the crazy ones; the people who have kept me alive and lifted me up with love again and again; the ones who have laughed with me and fought by my side.

Hot tramps, I love you so.

INTRODUCTION

SUGAR TOOTH I

I'VE BEEN THINKING ABOUT GIRLS A LOT RECENTLY.
And sugar. I know there's a sweet tooth, but is there actually a
girl tooth? A specific craving living in the mouths and pussies of
cunt-lovin' women, kicking in after unspecified periods of de
facto heterosexuality due to monogamous boy-girl commitment
or unlucky circumstance?

If only a girl tooth were as easy to satisfy as the desire for a
cookie, a big gooey brownie, or a bowl of creamy rice pudding. If
only we could acknowledge it for what it is—an irrational, period-
ic craving. A hormonal surge, perhaps. All I know is that suddenly
beautiful women are *everywhere.* They are magic in their summer
dresses, all pinned-up hair and long brown monkey arms. The
heat slows and simmers every motion they make, concentrating

SWEET

every precious step and gesture into exquisite reduction. And my girl tooth throbs piteously, despite the fact that I'm happy with my boyfriend and do not wish a change.

YOU CAN MAKE a sugar scrub by blending equal parts white sugar and olive oil, scenting the resulting gritty paste with any essential oil you like. You can take your scrub into the shower and abrade every square inch of your skin, sloughing away all the old, dead cells—emerging brand-new, raw, tender, pink as steamed shrimp. The sugar crystals sand your rough edges away, but the olive oil stays on you like Vaseline on a burn, a protective slime-coat under which your poor, scraped skin repairs, desperately soft. The fragrance remains throughout your day, a persistent ghost living in the seams of your clothes and the folds of your skin—armpits, knees, inner elbows. You'd better like the scent you pick, or all day long you'll be inhaling the aroma of something not quite right.

MY LAST GIRLFRIEND was a bright-eyed Midwesterner, a high-altitude settler used to dry winters, power failures, and impassably snowy streets banked with dirty drifts of ice. She was defiantly short, wide-hipped, wide-mouthed, and generously busted, with a river of black hair flowing nearly to her waist and a collection of snow boots in six different colors. She was pure pioneer stock: a wood chopper, a water carrier, a cow milker, a believer in bulk buyers' clubs and Jiffy corn muffin mixes, a sock mender, a down-to-earth American woman. She had tiny grasping doll hands with pragmatically short nails. She had advanced degrees, achieved methodically, and a small business, developed shrewdly. She owned her own winter-tight residence, painted in interior jewel tones of red and purple, housing herself and her two sleek and pampered cats.

I met her on the Internet. Later, when my book tour took me to her big, square state, she collected me at the airport and—generously and without question—opened her home to me. Everything in her orbit was miniature, from her tiny car (plastered with political stickers) to the little wooden TV trays on which she ate her dinners. Everything she owned was perfectly scaled for her, and I felt like a long-legged interloper, continually crashing into her things and bruising my shins against low, sneaky tables. My feet practically hung off her bed. I towered over her—cartoonishly tattooed, bleached blond—my tropical coloration completely wrong for constant icy wind and single-digit temperature. I didn't own a single pair of snow boots (though I brought two pairs of strappy heels that languished in my suitcase unworn, as if a Midwestern winter were a joke of questionable taste that could be called off at will).

When I held her and she laid her cheek against my heart I felt like some monstrous Frankenstein's creation—simultaneously protective in my will and inadvertently destructive in the nature of my being. I borrowed her sable makeup brushes and gave them back stained. She cleaned them, reformed their tips, and laid them to dry on a soft washcloth. I broke her drinking glasses. She swept up the shards with a tiny, hand-size brush and a miniature dustpan. I was afraid to touch her expensive stereo and avoided her jewelry like Kryptonite.

She was so beautiful and tiny, there were times I was ter-

SWEET

rified of touching her. I was afraid she'd turn out to be just as fragile as the other items I'd ruined.

SHE GRILLED ME steak on her miniature balcony Hibachi, after matter-of-factly sweeping six inches of snow from its cover with her forearm. In her part of the country, six inches of snow was nothing. I tried to explain that in Seattle, two inches of melting slush effectively shut the entire municipality down, closing bus routes and schools and inspiring much joyous hoarding of candles, bottled water, and liquor. She laughed uncertainly as she turned the oozing steaks over—were Washingtonians really that effete? I thought of the high heels I'd packed: *Yes, we were.*

From her I learned the word *frizzante*, a term more ordinarily applied to sparkling wine, but in this case describing the slight sizzle on the tongue you experience when you eat fresh tomatoes that have almost, but not quite, gone bad. Before they rot they turn to sugar, and the gas released during their transformation into garbage gives their flesh an astonishing, transient depth of flavor, redolent of saltwater and smoky honey. I devoured her homemade bruschetta, and it was as if I'd never eaten a tomato before in my life, only pale-orange mealy-textured supermarket proxies. I was speechlessly grateful: Whatever we didn't finish that night would have to be thrown away.

And later that evening with my tongue between her thighs, I thought again of the quicksilver intoxication of *frizzante*, and the frenzy of consumption such a rare sensation inspires.

SUGAR TOOTH I

GIRLS LOVE SWEET things, for the most part, and I romanced her the best I could, padding around her unfamiliar kitchen in pajama pants and a borrowed pair of woolly socks. Her culinary staples were bewilderingly different from mine: She didn't own molasses or cornmeal, but she had three different kinds of olive oil and five bottles of flavored vinegar. We compromised, giggling, and made salads.

A blizzard shut the city down for several days, but we were in no danger of running out of food: She had a dry-goods larder full of food put by for just such occasions. Room-temperature champagne left on her balcony for a quarter of an hour returned to us almost frozen, like the watery slush most Seattleites call *snow*. We drank it as her cats circulated, arching and flexing, excited by the big lacy flakes that blew into her living room from outside.

IF YOU HAVE a long afternoon of nothing but time, and you want to make treats for a beautiful girl, try making faux chocolate truffles.

You will need a saucepan, a heatproof bowl, a couple bags of chocolate chips (semisweet, milk, white, even peanut butter!— whatever you have on hand), some whipping cream, and any booze or flavored liqueur you like.

Fill the saucepan about halfway with water and heat the water to boiling. Turn the heat down so that the water is simmering, and put the heatproof bowl on top of the saucepan. It should be big enough so that the bowl kind of sits on top of the pan; ideally, the bottom of the bowl will be just *above* the simmering water, not submerged in it. You're jerry-rigging a double-

140

boiler, which is a fancy piece of specialized kitchen equipment that's basically just a bowl over a saucepan.

Pour one bag of chocolate chips into the bowl and allow them to melt. This will take a long time, but you'll know they're melting when they get shiny and your kitchen starts smelling like a giant Hershey's bar. You can stir them with a clean, dry metal spoon to hasten the melting, but be very careful not to get any water droplets or detritus into the melting chocolate. Chocolate, by nature, is temperamental—treat her like a lady and she'll make you feel like a million bucks, but disrespect her by getting her wet or stirring her with a dirty spoon and she'll form sullen, gritty lumps that are impossible to melt (or sweet-talk) away.

Once your chips have melted into one molten chocolate mass, stir stir stir. You're *tempering* the chocolate—exposing it to air, allowing it to breathe like wine. Professional chocolatiers sometimes have pieces of equipment specifically for tempering that look like the embodiment of premenstrual fantasy: Rivers of warm chocolate—gallons and gallons of it—spill into chocolate lagoons, circulating lazily at a steady temperature. Chocolatiers know that chocolate can't be rushed, can't be pushed.

So stir gently until your chocolate is glossy, then remove the bowl from the top of the saucepan. Add a few tablespoons of whipping cream slowly, stirring constantly until the chocolate and cream kind of puff up together, like nougat or marshmallow. Be sparing—remember, you can always pour in more cream but you can't take it away once it's been added. At this point, you can add a few drops of vanilla or a splash of liqueur: Grand Marnier, Kahlúa, Baileys Irish Cream—even peppermint schnapps can be nice, if you like York Peppermint Patties (and who doesn't?).

Once your chocolate has turned from molten liquid into light, nougaty solid and you've added boozy deliciousness (or not), stop stirring it and refrigerate your truffle mix for four hours.

Watch the snow, pet the kitties, and drink more icy champagne.

After your chocolate has fully chilled through, take it out and quickly roll it into balls, using your fingers. Refrigerate the chocolate balls. Try not to eat them all—that's like polishing off all the cookie dough without baking a single batch, decadent but ultimately disappointing.

Now: Make your double-boiler again using a clean, dry bowl on top. Pour in the second package of chocolate morsels, and melt them the way you melted the first portion. Stir till your chocolate shines like patent leather.

Now take your chilled chocolate balls out of the fridge and use two forks to dip them in the warm liquid chocolate until evenly coated, one at a time. Remove the coated truffles to a baking sheet lined with wax paper, if you have it (but I never do—a naked baking sheet is fine). Return them to the fridge until the chocolate coatings are firm and solid.

By this time it is night, and the snow has muffled all street sounds, and you're safe and warm and a little buzzed, wrapped in a quilt on the couch with your girl. She kisses you and her tongue is surprisingly cold from the icy champagne, like a finger running down your spine. Your own mouth tastes of cream and chocolate.

Sweets for the sweet.

SWEET

SUGAR TOOTH 2

IT WAS TOO MUCH.

It was too much sweetness, too much care. Too much love. I couldn't breathe. I felt like a rangy alley cat, scooped up and groomed into humiliated misery—a pretty bow and a tinkly bell around my neck proclaiming my fealty. I felt conquered. I lapped up her cream, but I couldn't get comfortable sleeping at her feet.

Also, it was complicated: I'd been seeing a man in Seattle. It had been casual and my girl had known all about it—until all of a sudden it *wasn't* casual, and I had to do the right thing, which was the most horrible thing I could possibly do to someone who had trusted me to do no harm.

I broke her heart into approximately ten million tiny pieces. It was a clumsy murder, and I was ashamed. Insipid words dribbled down my chin like warm milk as I extricated myself from something most people would have killed for: a good woman, a warm hearth, a *home*. All of that was offered to me, and I turned it down. I could have had a different kind of vinaigrette for my salad every night of the week.

Then I took my strappy heels and slunk back to Seattle, dazed and culpable, secretly relieved to leave the wintry Midwest to its own bluster.

AT HOME I baked white Betty Crocker cake and frosted it with canned chocolate icing. I ate chunks of it from my hands, licking my fingers.

I drank champagne, but it wasn't the same. There was something unpleasantly fey about champagne refrigerated to a civilized chill, instead of barbarically semi-frozen. I drank half the bottle and poured the rest out.

WHEN YOU NEED to feel busy—creative, instead of destructive—

—when you need to get your hands dirty—

—when you need to feel scoured clean after a blundering slaughter—

—and, when you need the cracked-out mood elevation that only a large amount of sugar can provide—

—that's when you make yourself a big stack of corncakes for breakfast.

Well, that's what *I* do, anyway. It beats starting a lonely morning with last night's champagne.

THIS RECIPE LIVES in my scrapbook, annotated "Noah—January 1993." Noah was my best friend in high school. We cooked together constantly, when we weren't dropping acid and listening to Pink Floyd. 1993 was a year of good food and lots of glassy-eyed giggling, till Noah set his parents' kitchen on fire melting saltpeter into sugar to make a low-tech smoke bomb. At that point we stuck to dropping acid. It seemed safer.

I believe Noah adapted this recipe from his copy of *The Joy of Cooking*, but I can't swear to it. So many recipes are like playing Telephone—one person whispers his or her recipe to the next person, who whispers his or her version to the next person, and so on down the line. I don't want to look this recipe up because I like the Telephone version I've got.

Some days it's good to remember that somebody loved you enough to whisper in your ear.

START WITH ONE cup of cornmeal, a quarter cup of sugar, and a dash of salt in a small mixing bowl. Boil water and pour one cup of hot water over the cornmeal. Stir it, cover the bowl with a plate, and set aside for ten minutes.

In another small bowl, beat one egg and a half cup of half-and-half or cream. Add about a quarter stick of melted butter or a few tablespoons of bacon fat. If you don't have either on hand, use canola or any other mild oil—melted Crisco is fine. Beat the egg, the cream, and the butter or bacon fat, then add the mixture to the dry ingredients in the other bowl and blend.

Add a half cup of white flour and two teaspoons baking powder. Mix with very few strokes. The batter should be barely

145

blended and lumpy. Resist the urge to beat the hell out of it. This will not make you feel better.

Heat a skillet on medium, or a little hotter, until a few drops of water flicked from your fingertips appear to skip across the base of the pan. Toss a chunk of butter and a little bacon fat into the skillet and allow them to melt together (or just use canola, or Crisco—a good game of Telephone is always open to interpretation).

Use a measuring cup or ladle to spoon pancake-size circles of batter into the hot pan. Let your corncakes rest until their visible surfaces are covered in air bubbles. Don't poke or molest them. Don't squash them. Don't flip them too early. Wait for the bubbles. They mean the baking powder's working to give your cakes an airy, crispy texture.

When they're all covered with air bubbles, use a heat-safe spatula to flip them over. The second sides should cook faster than the first sides. Don't let your babies burn.

Once your cakes are all browned, put them on a plate and layer them with fruit preserves or honey or molasses. You can butter the layers if you want. You can top the whole stack with a blob of plain whole-milk yogurt, like whipped cream on a corn sundae. You can be fancy and just sprinkle your cakes with a little powdered sugar and lemon juice. Remember what you like best, because someday you may want to whisper it into someone's ear.

This recipe yields enough for two people, but if your heart needs repair and you're eating corncakes all by yourself, you may find that the entire batch is only barely enough.

SWEET

PUMPKIN PIE

MEN LOVE THE AROMA OF PUMPKIN PIE THE WAY RICH ladies adore the scent of Chanel No. 5.

They're drawn to it—it magnetizes them, braces them, gets their dicks hard. Don't believe me? Seriously: Ask Dr. Alan Hirsch, who studied scent and arousal in the late '90s as the director of Chicago's Smell & Taste Treatment and Research Foundation. He determined that out of all the fragrances tested, men became most aroused by the spicy sweet scent of pumpkin pie combined with lavender.[1] He figured this out by measuring—ahem—"penile blood flow." (I hope he wore latex gloves.)

---

1. Women liked the odors of fresh cucumber and—get this—Good & Plenties, those gross cold-capsule-shaped licorice punishment candies favored by batty old ladies and movie theaters! No wonder men can't figure us out!

The lavender part makes a certain amount of sense—after all, lavender is a relaxing scent, and you usually have to be relaxed in order to be turned on. If you're smelling lavender you're probably in a clean, safe, homelike environment—like Bed Bath & Beyond, or an upscale lingerie boutique. It's understandable to draw a big arrow from feeling safe and relaxed to feeling randy. I tend to get turned on in shopping malls more than I'd like to admit, especially when high school is out and all the surly young men lean against the Orange Julius stand like a jailbait chorus line.

But lavender mixed with the scent of pumpkin pie—I just don't know about that. Maybe there's some crucial genetic information on the Y chromosome, positing that women adept at pie baking also tend toward success in the equally time-consuming and messy arenas of gestation and childbirth. Or maybe men are just pigs for pie of all kinds, as evinced by two of my favorite lip-smacking, elbow-nudging terms used primarily by men of a certain sort to describe the female pudendum: *cherry pie* and *hair pie*. Pumpkin pie no longer seems like such a stretch.

Frankly, if I thought it would get me laid, I'd roll myself in coconut, dip my ass in chocolate, and call myself a macaroon.

IF YOU WANT to know the truth, I adore smelling like pretty much anything edible (with the exception of fish and cheese, which usually means I've skipped a shower). In my bathroom cabinet right now are the following products:

- Neapolitan Shea Body Butter, in Chocolate Souffle

- Desert Essence Organics Hand and Body Lotion, in Vanilla Chai

SWEET

- Skintimates Shave Gel, in Raspberry Rain

- The Body Shop Body Butter, in Blueberry

- Jaqua Foaming Caramel Cappuccino Hydrating
  Shower Syrup (which wins the prize for tempting
  dessert-loving buyers with a trifecta of deliciousness—
  caramel, cappuccino, and, in a brilliant stroke of
  advertising genius, *syrup*)

I'm not even mentioning the specific products I use for their fragrances alone (Vanilla Fantasy Fragrance Body Spray, Luxe Pink Grapefruit Body Mist, and Demeter Sugar Cookie Cologne Spray). Basically, my bathroom smells like a confectionary: If I took more than one bath a day, I'd probably give myself diabetes.

But the product I love the most—out of all of my sugary-sweet lotions and potions—is my Philosophy 3-in-1 Shampoo, Conditioner, and Shower Gel. Why? Because it gets me laid. Why? Because its scent is Pumpkin Pie.

Not just Pumpkin, mind you. Pumpkin *Pie*.

Yes, *that* scent. Cinnamon, cloves, nutmeg, and pureed pumpkin, baked together in a golden crust. That's the product I make sure to use (in combination with a little lavender oil sprinkled on my pillow) when I'm trying to get lucky and my intended purveyor of sexual bliss carries both X and Y chromosomes.[2]

Which brings me to one of the many charms of my

---

2. For women, I should really invest in some Good & Plenty—scented shower gel, the lack of which may explain my chronic inability to date women with any regularity—a mysterious gender inequality that certainly can't be ascribed to my chronic, joyous use of the terms *cherry pie* and *hair pie*.

pumpkin-pie-scented Philosophy 3-in-1 Shampoo, Conditioner, and Shower Gel: the recipe on the bottle.

One of the tastiest conceits of Philosophy—an expensive brand with deceptively simple packaging—is that its food-scented products nearly always have recipes on them, for whatever food it is that the shampoo or bubble bath or hair conditioner or body lotion smells like. The recipes pretty much sell the products: You may not have time to make an angel food cake but you can sure as hell take a shower and smell like one, and isn't that almost as good? Plus, taking a shower won't add unwanted angel food poundage. Thus, you can have your cake and (not) eat it, too. Sheer marketing inspiration, using recipes women will never follow to sell products they'll use to smell like the delectable foods they shun! It makes my head spin (or maybe that's hunger, because Lord knows I smell like an Italian bakery, though I haven't had a piece of angel food cake in months).

Because I was offended at the idea of a recipe *not meant to be followed*, under the assumption that most women would rather smell like a pie than eat one,[3] I determined to make pumpkin pie from the recipe on my Philosophy 3-in-1 bottle. I'd discover whether the recipe was merely window dressing, meaningless text designed solely to sell the shampoo inside the bottle, or whether some pie-loving bigwig at Philosophy actually took care to make sure that the recipe resulted in a firm, creamy, spiced pumpkin custard, snug in a flaky casing of crust. Every time I used my Pumpkin Pie 3-in-1, I wondered. I had to find out.

And if my sudden pie-baking frenzy got me laid, even

---

3. And despite the fact that my favorite pies are, in fact, *cherry* and *hair*.

SWEET

better. I had to admit the fringe benefits were potentially excellent: a scrumptious dessert *and* a few toe-curling orgasms? Even a mediocre pie and a mild, vibrator-fueled spasm were better than *no* pie and *no* sex. I couldn't *not* find out.

My Ojibwe beau obtained canned pumpkin puree for me at the local tribal commodities distribution center (so yes, in a staggeringly colonial move, I actually *stole food from Native Americans*). He had been apprised of my project in advance and didn't feel morally conflicted about the appropriation of pumpkin for his lily-white girlfriend—or maybe he was just thinking with his dick, anticipating a cinnamon-scented kitchen and a randy pie-romp. Either way, I figured I could reduce my karmic debt for the theft if I made sure that my beau ate most of the pie—that way, at least, most of the food would be going to its intended recipient.

I bought two frozen piecrusts for $1.99 on sale at Safeway. I had evaporated milk and all the spices I needed. I sent Beau to the store for eggs—"*jumbo* ones," I specified. "Not the little puny ones." I wanted the pumpkin custard to be rich and eggy, falling apart tenderly at the merest touch of a dessert fork.

For legal reasons I can't give the recipe here: It's the property of Philosophy, and I don't want to get sued. But you can buy some of its Pumpkin Pie 3-in-1 Shampoo, Conditioner, and Shower Gel for the recipe right there on the front of the bottle. I can report that I followed the recipe to the letter, refraining from doubling the spices the way I ordinarily do with any pumpkin pie recipe (though in the interest of full disclosure, I must note that I was unable to resist adding generous pinches of allspice and nutmeg). The recipe instructed me to cook the pie at 425 degrees for 40 minutes, or "until desired consistency is achieved." I like a firm pie myself, so I added twenty minutes to the cooking time.[4]

And . . . ?

You know, Philosophy pumpkin pie is *okay*. It's a perfectly decent, perfectly usable recipe for a dark, full-bodied pumpkin pie, thus answering my question about whether the text was simply for show, to sell a product, or actually meant as instructions for something you'd enjoy putting in your mouth for pleasure and sustenance. It works very well, actually.

And by *works* I mean that the shit got me laid like nobody's business. I didn't even have to touch up the lavender scent on my pillow after the first romp. (It was wedged under my ass, anyway.)

So thank you, Dr. Alan Hirsch. Thank you very much. Your search for pure scientific knowledge has given me the subliminal power of seduction I've always wanted—the olfactory tools to fight dirty in the pursuit of gettin' dirty.

---

4. A helpful hint I learned from Beau's father, a consummate pie maker in his own right: Make a tinfoil ring to protect the crust of your pie from overbaking by laying your pie tin upside down on a sheet of foil. Cut a circle in the foil about an inch larger than the pin tin, then fold the cutout circle of foil in half and cut a smaller circle in its middle (about five inches in diameter or so). You now have an open circle of foil that you can press gently over the edges of your piecrust to keep it from getting too brown during extended baking. This method beats the pants off of my previous method of foiling, which involved strips of foil that chronically fell off and didn't provide even crust coverage.

BABY RUTH MAN

I ONCE WORKED AS A MODEL AT A RUN-DOWN LITTLE establishment known as Butterscotch's Live Lingerie Adult Tanning. It was a place where men went to masturbate in front of disaffected women who more or less hated them, or at the gentlest extreme, viewed them as giant toddlers requiring constant supervision to prevent them from contaminating our workplace with shit, sweat, come, and saliva. We ordered them to sit on towels and come into washcloths. We opened and shut all the doors to prevent their hands from coming into contact with the doorknobs. We kept Lysol and latex gloves handy and used them whenever a customer made physical contact with anything—the doors, the walls, the carpet, the toilet, etc. One model I knew kept a can of Lysol under the couch in her showroom in case a customer attempted to paw her with his baby-oil- and pre-come-slicked hands as she posed for him.

"First I'd spray him in the eyes," she explained. "Then I'd spray my skin to disinfect it."

I admired her sensible attention to timing: first his eyes, then her skin. She'd be clean as a whistle before he recovered from his Country Fresh teargassing. Pre-come didn't carry as many viruses as actual come—but any time you had a man handling his own cock, you had to worry about skin-shed nasties like herpes. We watched them and made sure that their hands only came into contact with the bottles of baby oil we provided, their washcloths, the towels they sat on, and their own bodies. Our worst nightmare was a customer exiting his room after his session unaccompanied, smearing come and lube and ass-juice onto every doorknob between his showroom and the street.

You'd think that in such a filthy environment none of us would eat. But you'd be wrong. We gobbled takeout food like lumberjacks, ordering Indian food and sushi and greasy American-style Chinese food swimming in sweet red pineapple sauce, then ran to the convenience store on the corner for junk food desserts like squashy, plastic-tasting MoonPies and sleeves of Lorna Doone shortbread cookies. We were hungry, and for the first time most of us were making enough to afford prepared food. It felt fancy. Our food arrived steaming hot in Styrofoam clamshells and little paper boxes accompanied by napkins and plastic cutlery, and we ate it in frantic gulps between seeing our customers, like pathologists casually lunching on sandwiches between autopsies. It was a little gross at first, but eventually we all learned to compartmentalize and could separate our disgust at watching a customer finger-fuck his own shit-encrusted asshole from our delight in the hot, delicious food waiting for us after our shows. We just sprayed some Lysol on the couch where Shit-Ass had been sitting, replaced the towel, washed our hands, and got over it.

We didn't get fat from our constant feasting because our jobs required constant motion, posing and dancing in high heels. We ate a lot of cake, imported from the supermarket bakery down the street from Butterscotch's. We ordered a lot of pizzas. One girl bought cans of frosting at the convenience store, which she'd eat with a spoon over the course of her shifts. She particularly liked the vanilla kind with rainbow sprinkles. We were gluttons for salt, chocolate, and sugar. Someone was always just about to have her period, so we blamed contact PMS for our cravings.

Sometimes we even ate in shows. One customer liked to bring in Baby Ruth bars, which he enjoyed watching his model devour as he masturbated. "Slower," he'd groan, yanking his own crank savagely. I learned to take my time—first deliberately unwrapping the candy bar, then sniffing and licking it, then finally taking tiny, hesitant, ladylike bites of the bar as he arched and unloaded into his washcloth. He always brought Baby Ruths—never other kinds. He was always good for a $20 tip if you let the chocolate coating melt enough so that when you nuzzled it, you'd give yourself a big brown clown-mouth. Once, I took a bite and then playfully opened my mouth, allowing him to see the chunk of half-chewed candy on my tongue. He exploded in a fierce, bucking orgasm as I shut my mouth and swallowed. That time I got a $40 tip.

It was a long time before I caught on to Baby Ruth Man's deal, and when I did, I kind of wished I hadn't. But when you get

BABY RUTH MAN

down and dirty for pay, you have to have an encyclopedic knowledge of the grotesque to do your job—and if you want to do your job well, a certain instinctive appreciation for filth will serve you well. Sitting in judgment rarely pays a working girl's rent.

IT WAS FRIDAY night and I was working with Lenore. We were in the lounge, lazily ruining what remained of our extra-large pepperoni, sausage, and green pepper pizza by picking the toppings off and popping the cheese-covered meat morsels into our mouths. Nobody would want to eat the resulting slices of tomato-sauce-covered crust, but we didn't care. We'd each made more than $100 and were feeling decadent. We'd throw the stripped slices away and buy another pizza when we wanted one.

The buzzer went off, indicating a customer had entered our lobby. I was up, so I squinted at the closed-circuit monitor to attempt to discern the identity of the person taking up space in our front office. Was he a newbie or a regular? I couldn't see. The cheap monitor was impossible and tended to display colors as their own photographic negatives. For instance, if you walked out wearing a black dress, it would appear pale gray. You couldn't identify customers by their features, but often their body shape and the way they held themselves would offer clues. A man who came in confidently and sat right down was usually a repeat offender. A guy who stood nervously, hovering by the door, was usually new. It wasn't rocket science. I mostly used the monitor to make sure that anyone entering in the lobby wasn't holding a chainsaw or any other visible weapon. Since my guy wasn't, I slipped on my seven-inch platform heels and prepared to go meet him.

"Who is it?" asked Lenore, belching. I smelled green pepper all the way over on my side of the room.

"Gross!" I yelped, pulling my tits up and resettling them in their bra cups for maximum cleavage.

Lenore answered me by cutting a prim fart. She was a heart-stoppingly beautiful girl with silky black Bettie Page bangs, but once you got to know her you realized the bangs were a wig and that underneath her fragile loveliness Lenore had the comic sensibilities of a long-haul trucker. Long satin gloves hid her tattoos, and up close you could see the scars of piercings past in her nose, eyebrows, and chin.

"One of these days you're going to shit your pants doing that," I said. "I don't know. I think he's a regular. He's just standing there." I fluffed my own wig—my favorite red Cleopatra model, bought at the Halloween store for $22—and doused my exposed chest and neck with Vanilla Fantasy body spray. I squirted a puff of vanilla spray Lenore's way. She squealed at the cold droplets that coated her skin with the nostril-curling scent of cotton candy.

I staggered down the hall, my feet acclimating to my shoes, and by the time I reached the lobby, I was making my way over the snagged, uneven shag carpet more or less smoothly. If you caught your heel in one of the bits of pulled-out shag, you'd fall over. We all learned to pick our feet up like show ponies when we had our work shoes on—taking a dive in front of a customer was embarrassing, and could be disgusting if they attempted to assist you up with their postsession semen-smeared paws. It was much better to stay upright and out of reach.

When I reached the locked door to the lobby, I paused. Did I still smell like a fat, sweaty Sicilian man's garlicky armpit from

BABY RUTH MAN

the pizza, or was the vanilla spray heavy enough to cover my gustatory excess? We hadn't even eaten the salad that had come with our pie—we'd just picked off the pepperoncini and the little diced chunks of salami, dunked them in the vinaigrette dressing, and eaten them with our fingers, completely ignoring the torn baby spinach leaves beneath. My own tongue tasted sour to me, furred with garlic and balsamic vinegar and meat grease.

Stepping into the lobby and getting my first real-life look at the customer, I smiled. It was Baby Ruth Man! And while I was already quite full from the pizza, a little dessert wasn't beyond the realm of possibility. I had always liked Baby Ruths—the peanuts were a good foil for the spongy nougat, and they were chewy enough to last longer than an all-nougat fluff-bar like Three Musketeers. My smile became genuine. Baby Ruth Man had saved me a trip to the convenience store!

"Hi, darling," I purred. "You ready for your show?"

Baby Ruth Man nodded, smiling. He handed me a small brown paper bag that I knew contained one king-size Baby Ruth bar and a dated receipt. We insisted upon the receipt to make sure the candy was freshly purchased and hadn't just been sitting around Baby Ruth Man's house getting fondled or licked in anticipation.

I reached into the bag and checked the receipt. He always bought his candy in different places, and it was fun to see where he'd made his latest buy. Today he'd shopped at the supermarket down the street where we bought our cake, meaning that in all likelihood, his visit was unplanned. When he schlepped his candy all the way from West Seattle and the receipt was time-stamped before 8:00 AM, we assumed he'd bought his Baby

Ruth bar before work and spent his day in a pleasant erotic haze, imagining his model peeling the wrapper back and taking her first hesitant bite.

What was it about Baby Ruths in particular, though? Why would no other candy bar do? Were Baby Ruths just somehow inherently sexier than other kinds of candy? Or did he have an erotic fixation on someone from his past who favored them? None of us knew. He saw all of us indiscriminately but never varied his candy bar.

"We're good to go, sugar," I said. "Follow me."

I led Baby Ruth Man back down the hall from where I'd emerged and waved him into the showroom I'd claimed at the beginning of my shift.

"Go ahead and get comfortable, baby," I said. "I'm going to put on something sexy for you—be right back." I waved the paper bag containing the Baby Ruth at him temptingly, then shut the door between us.

"Who is it?" asked Lenore, as I returned to the lounge. She was sprawled indolently across the couch like a well-fed lion basking on a sun-warmed rock. Her belly strained against her evening dress, giving her a rakish knocked-up air. I smelled sulphurous onion-farts.

"Baby Ruth Man," I said.

"What the fuck is up with him?"

It was an old conversation. Baby Ruth Man was inscrutable, and no matter how precisely we shared with each other the details of our sessions with him, none of us knew anything more about him than his candy preference and the shape and size of his penis.

"I don't know," I said. "But I kind of wish I hadn't eaten so much pizza." I eyed the denuded slices lying haphazardly in the grease-stained pizza box. Suddenly I had to fight the urge to fling myself on the unoccupied sofa across the room, to kick off my shoes and loll like a sybarite until my stomach felt a little less vacuum-packed.

"Twenty-buck tip," said Lenore, shrugging.

I didn't mention the forty I'd made the last time I'd seen him.

"Yeah," I said. "And all the Baby Ruth you can eat."

Lenore giggled, then flopped over on her side. "Fuck, I'm full," she groaned. "Glad it isn't me."

I WENT INTO the dressing room, stripped off my dress, and exchanged my comfortable cotton drawers for a flashy thong, as brittle with sequins and snaky straps as a stiletto shoe. I added a lace slip, then sniffed my own armpits. I was a little garlicky, but with any luck Baby Ruth Man would be so revved up he'd come before I had to get within smell-distance of him.

Once properly attired for my modeling session, I glanced down at the paper bag of Baby Ruth on the makeup counter. No need to put on more lip gloss—he preferred melted chocolate to fruit-flavored shine. The chocolate-smeared mouth meant a $20 tip for sure, but it was hard to get the waxy chocolate coating sufficiently soft in the time allotted. Sometimes you'd end up rubbing the candy bar on your skin so hard it was painful.

Suddenly, I had an idea. I opened the Baby Ruth and put in on a paper plate. Then I slid the plate into the dorm-size microwave oven we used for leftovers and bags of popcorn. I gave it thirty

SWEET

seconds, then thirty more. When I pulled the hot plate out of the microwave the bar was steaming slightly, and when I prodded it, chocolate coated my fingertip. Perfect! Baby Ruth Man would get the chocolate clown-mouth of his dreams! I pictured three twenties laid out neatly on the table at the conclusion of my show—my tip, earned by my own candy-bar-wrangling ingenuity!

I hurried to my showroom holding the plate of hot Baby Ruth. I had to admit, it smelled good. It was nice to be inhaling something other than Lenore's pungent gas.

Did Baby Ruth Man give out those mini fun-size Baby Ruths for Halloween? I wondered. Or would that be an uncomfortable collision of erotic fantasy and real life? I wondered if he even ate Baby Ruths himself. He'd never seemed motivated by a sense of the candy being delicious—it was the spectacle of his models wallowing in messy brown gluttony that seemed to get his dick hard. I suddenly wondered if he only brought Baby Ruths because they were so widely available—even the smallest convenience stores tended to stock them.

I entered the showroom. Baby Ruth Man was naked, sitting cooperatively on the bath-towel-covered sofa. His penis was curled in his lap like an old sock. When he saw me holding the steaming paper plate of Baby Ruth, his back stiffened. *"Yes,"* he moaned.

I set the hot plate on my chair, since I didn't want to put it on the floor and the table was off-limits, that being the place where the bottles of baby oil used by the customers were stored. The idea of eating anything that close to communal cock- and ass-lube made me shudder. I didn't even like Windexing the oil-smeared glass-topped table in latex gloves.

BABY RUTH MAN

The bumpy, peanutty Baby Ruth was still steaming, and the smell of melted chocolate filled the room. I put in my CD, turned it down low, and set the plastic kitchen timer next to the boom box for fifteen minutes. When it went off, his show would be over. Hopefully, the deluxe, hot Baby Ruth clown-mouth I'd contrived would shave five long minutes or more off his show time. Like short-order cooks, our motto was *Turn and burn, baby:* We got paid by the orgasm, not by the minute, and it was one to a customer.

Baby Ruth Man was already stroking himself. "Pretend you just found it," he breathed. I was used to customers who wanted to call the shots, micromanaging every gesture and line of dialogue for their sessions. Most clients preferred their models to improvise as long as they eventually stripped down to their bras and G-strings, leaving them free to masturbate without having to direct the action. But customers with specific fetishes tended to be rigid about what they wanted in their performances, and it didn't pay to argue. It was best to comply, within reason. Butterscotch's wasn't Lee Strasburg's Actors Studio—we were being paid to pander, not to emote.

I turned around and let my gaze fall on the candy bar on my chair. "Oh my goodness," I said primly, pressing one hand to my cheek. I looked around. "Did somebody leave this here?" I approached the Baby Ruth with trepidation.

"Smell it," urged Baby Ruth Man. "*Smell it.*"

I stepped out of my lacy slip casually and knelt at my chair, as if genuflecting. Suddenly remembering the pizza I'd eaten earlier, I sucked my gut in sharply. "My . . . what an aroma," I said. I glanced at Baby Ruth Man for direction, but his eyes were squeezed shut in bliss. "My! What an aroma!" I said again. "It

SWEET

smells so . . . " *Good? Bad?* I didn't know which way to go. Did he want me to like it? To hate it? Baby Ruth Man wasn't providing any clues. His masturbation was rhythmic and brisk.

I took a chance. " . . . so *good!*"

Baby Ruth Man whimpered.

"I think I want to eat some of this delicious candy bar," I said.

Baby Ruth Man frowned slightly, so I tried again.

"Do I want to eat some of this—" I stopped. Maybe it would be better to cut directly to the action.

"Mmmmmmm," I said. Then I stuck my tongue out and licked the length of the bar like a Popsicle. I turned to Baby Ruth Man, showing him the melted chocolate coating my tongue. I'd licked off nearly the entire coating on the top of the bar. Peanuts were visible, and underneath those, glistening nougat.

I rubbed my lips on the candy bar, smearing chocolate around my mouth. It felt yielding and warm, like fragrant heated lotion—why hadn't I thought to microwave the bar before? This was genius! I made a mental note to tell my coworkers of my discovery, so when they did shows for Baby Ruth Man they wouldn't have to rub their skin raw trying to get visible chocolate on their lips.

"Eat it," Baby Ruth Man urged. I glanced at the kitchen timer. We had ten more minutes. This was going to be a cakewalk. He was almost orgasming already! I could afford to torture him a little, just for fun.

"Ooh, I don't know," I said coyly. "I'm not sure about that . . . " I sucked one chocolate-coated finger thoughtfully. "I don't think I'm really that hungry."

Baby Ruth Man pounded his penis harder. "Please! Eat it!"

"Well . . . I guess one little bite wouldn't hurt. It's so nice and warm, after all." I licked my lips. "You won't tell anyone, will you?" Customers generally loved the idea of being complicit in their models' taboo-breaking behavior, no matter how tame or softcore. It made them feel like we were on the same team—two horny people united in mutual depravity. Didn't the classic *Playboy* pose feature a bunny-eared model bending over with a finger pressed to her lips in a playfully arch *shhh—don't tell* gesture? Customers loved to imagine that deep inside every woman was a heart of indiscriminate perversity. At Butterscotch's, it was our job to confirm that delusion.

I leaned forward, nuzzling the paper plate. Then, after a tantalizingly long pause, I took one single, feline bite of the softened bar. Salty peanuts, chocolate, and sticky-sweet nougat exploded across my palate as I chewed. I remembered not to swallow. Turning to Baby Ruth Man, I opened my mouth and showed him the mess on my tongue.

"Eat it! Eat—" and with that, he shot his candy-lovin' load into a clean washcloth.

I was done. Once you got them to a certain point in their arousal, their orgasms tended to happen quickly and inevitably. Baby Ruth Man knew I was going to eat the candy bar, because that was what I was being paid to do, and it was that surety that took him over the edge. My actualization of his request had only been a formality.

As I politely waited for his spasm to end, I swallowed the candy perfunctorily. Baby Ruth Man wasn't paying attention, so I didn't have to be sexy. It was good, but the taste of candy-bar-grade chocolate didn't go well with all the pizza I'd eaten. I burped a little chocolate-and-garlic-scented puff, then surreptitiously waved my hand to disperse the odor. I looked forward to wiping the chocolate off my lips, and to eating a few Tums.

I glanced at the cooling, nibbled candy bar on the chocolate-smeared paper plate. Then I looked again.

No fucking way.

But yes—the mystery of Baby Ruth Man had suddenly become completely clear to me, and, once known, the terrible information could not be suppressed or disavowed. I felt it as a physical weight in my poor swollen gut as I gazed at the mess on my chair.

The melted Baby Ruth's resemblance to fecal matter was undeniable.

The smears of chocolate on the plate were unmistakably shit-inspired. The size and the shape of the bar suddenly made absurd sense. Other candy bars were smooth and aerodynamically squared-off, like Tokyo supertrain coaches. Only Baby Ruth was organically round and bumpy.

The peanuts added a touch of realism.

Baby Ruth Man was paying to watch us eat shit.

That was his fantasy, anyway. The brown mess on our faces—the way he liked to watch us smell, then nibble—the fact that he'd frowned when I referred to the Baby Ruth as a candy bar. Of course! I felt like Isaac Newton, dive-bombed by the gravity of a single earthbound apple. My cheeks felt hot, and all of a sudden the chocolate around my mouth felt unendurably caked-on and muddy. I swore I could actually smell shit.

It wasn't that I was humiliated. No, I found it far more humiliating to pretend to be aroused by normal lingerie show customers, as if their uninspired yanking was somehow responsible for my own histrionic faked orgasm. *That* was humiliating. This was merely disgusting. Eating shit—who would get turned on by that? I felt a little self-righteous. I considered myself fairly kinky in my personal life, but I drew the line well before coprophagia. Baby Ruth Man was a great big shit-loving freak!

I couldn't wait to tell the other girls. I'd finally cracked the mystery of Baby Ruth Man. I felt like punching the air in triumph. *Case closed!*

"Pretend you just found it. . . ." Yeah—a steaming brown log! I'd found it, all right.

I excused myself to the dressing room, telling Baby Ruth Man to dress and to wait in the room for me so I could escort him out. I wiped every trace of the chocolate from my mouth, chin, and cheeks, put my dress back on, and knocked on the door of the showroom. Baby Ruth Man was dressed and ready to go. I glanced over his shoulder and noted the two twenties on the glass-topped table next to the couch. *Cheapskate,* I thought. The nibbled Baby Ruth log cooling on my chair looked unbelievably obscene on its paper plate, like a foul practical joke. I couldn't wait to trick Lenore into looking at it. "I really had to go," I planned on saying. "I couldn't wait till the show was over." I imagined her outraged screams with pleasure.

I saw Baby Ruth Man out of the lobby and onto the street, then I went back to the lounge and told Lenore about my discovery.

"I've got him figured out," I said.

Lenore looked up from her magazine. It was *Seventeen.* The cover model's eyes had been cut out, and someone had drawn a pentagram on her freshly scrubbed forehead. *Back to school!* the cover trumpeted. I figured going back to school as a Satanist probably wasn't what the editorial staff meant. The articles were probably about wearing plaid and patent leather Mary Janes, not sacrificing goats. Though, in these post-*Sassy* days, you never knew what angle the fashion magazines would try to gain "edgy" readership.

"Who?" she asked.

"Baby Ruth Man," I said. "I've got him figured out."

I told her everything. When I showed her the melted Ruth on the plate, she screamed satisfyingly. I knew I was right.

NEWS OF MY discovery—the cracking of Baby Ruth Man's mysterious code—swept through Butterscotch's like wildfire. Some girls were indignant and vowed not to take shows with him in the future. The older girls just shrugged and made mental notes to play up the shit-eating, poo-smearing scenario like the pros they were. I was in the latter camp—his shit fixation was gross, sure, but no more terrible or degrading than any of the other contortions we went through to make our customers come. Frankly, I preferred getting paid to eat microwaved candy to pretending to finger-bang my own pussy through the cotton gusset of my thong.

A few weeks later, after most of the Baby Ruth Man hubbub had died down, I bought a five-pound jumbo bag of fun-size Baby Ruths on my way to work and put them in a big bowl on top of the television set in the lounge. EAT ME, read the note I taped to the bowl. I wasn't sure if anyone would, though. Maybe Baby Ruths were forever ruined for the staff of Butterscotch's. Which would be a shame, because regardless of Baby Ruth Man's shit fixation, they were a damn good candy bar. Peanuts, chocolate, and nougat, blessed by a butterfly kiss of caramel—classic ingredients in lovely proportion, without any newfangled gimmickry or flashy sales hooks, named in sweet, old-fashioned sincerity for President Grover Cleveland's daughter. It wasn't Nestlé's fault that a lone pervert liked to use them as scatological masturbation material. Why couldn't he pick on Oh, Henry! instead? I didn't know anyone who liked those.

THE MINI BABY Ruths I left in the lounge were gone in two days. I ate a few myself. I was relieved to find that they were just as delicious as always.

AGAPAE

The Agape feast was one term used for certain meals celebrated by the early Christians. Agape is one of the Greek words for love, *particularly applied to selfless love or God's love for mankind, and so "agape feasts" are also referred to in English as "love-feasts."* —Wikipedia

Her milk is my shit; my shit is her milk. —Nirvana

THREE YEARS AGO, I had a customer who used to buy Dixie Cups of my pee.

I charged him $60 for the pee, and another $90 to watch him drink it. He wasn't a fiend or an obvious pervert: In fact, he was tall, clean, and handsome, with a neatly shaved head and educated elocution. My guess is that his girlfriends were proud to bring him home to their parents—he was a "good catch," a man running his own successful business, a home owner before the age of thirty. He worked hard and couldn't make time to see me often, but when he did, he had no trouble paying the sum I requested. He usually charged his sessions on his business Master-Card, writing my pee fee in carefully on the "Tip" line.

After the first few sessions during which I served him my warm pee in the disposable Dixie Cups I used for mouthwash, he began to arrive with an assortment of wineglasses for me. "It looks prettier," he said. "And there's no waxy aftertaste." I appreciated his sensitive palate, though I had to wonder how objectionable the taste of a wax-lined paper cup actually was to a man swirling his stripper's liquid waste on his tongue like Sémillon Blanc.

He explained the pee thing to me with fetching embarrassment: He'd lived in Europe for a few years, he said. Pee was "really big" over there—everyone was into it, and most of their pornography featured erotic peeing. Pee-drinking was far from uncommon. He'd had a British girlfriend, he claimed, who was particularly turned on by pee-play. She'd taught him to spread out a plastic shower curtain on the floor, then to carefully cover the plastic sheeting with an ordinary cotton bed sheet. The sheet, he said, trapped the pee and prevented it from running off the shower curtain onto the floor. Cleanup was a cinch: you simply threw both the shower curtain and the sheet into the bathtub and rinsed them both until they no longer smelled of urine. After that, you could run them through the washer, if you liked. You dried the sheet normally and hung the shower curtain over the shower rod to dry.

SWEET

I was impressed with his European girlfriend's trial-and-error ingenuity. It would have taken me a long time (and a lot of urine-sodden carpeting) to figure out the bed sheet thing, I knew. But then again, I wasn't a true pee aficionado. Maybe when you're into playing with piss, you have an instinct for how to contain it. Or maybe European porn flicks come with pragmatic instructions, like the San Francisco safe-sex videos starring the most terrifying lesbians we have here in America. Everyone always says that Europeans are more matter-of-fact than Americans about sex.

The one poetic indulgence my clean-cut pee customer allowed himself was that he loved referring to my pee as "golden nectar."

"Let me drink your golden nectar, Mistress," he begged. I felt like the Tree Top company. It was really amazing how much urine in a wineglass resembled apple juice, even down to its occasional cloudiness. And after one Day-Glo mishap, I tried to remember not to take B vitamins on the days I had my pee guy scheduled. I didn't want to ruin the golden hue of my nectar.

I wonder where Pee Guy is now. I hope that wherever he is, he's happily slurping up as much golden nectar as he wants. Maybe he's moved back to Europe, the land of freewheeling pee-lovers, and found a girlfriend who hates asparagus.

The thing about Pee Guy is that his kink doesn't seem that out of line to me. I mean, I'm not into peeing on anyone (or getting pissed on) in my personal life. I don't go out of my way to incorporate pee into my erotic activities—my only shower curtain hangs over my tub, and when I pee in the shower, I'm usually alone and just too lazy to get out and use the toilet. Peeing feels good to me—but it doesn't feel *orgasmically* good, and I'm okay with that.

It's not that I'm antipee, though—in fact, without even trying (or living in Europe), I'm sure I've swallowed my share. I don't baby-wipe my lover's crotch before I dive in: I'd rather risk a few drops of golden nectar in pursuit of my lover's sexual fluids than insist upon pee-free, laboratory-sterile conditions. I mean, they're *genitals*—peeing is what they *do*. They're supposed to! Cunts and cocks are only used for sex a tiny percent of the time—the rest of the time, they're the end points in your body's drainage system, nothing more. If you don't want to lick them, don't lick them, but don't get grossed out thinking about what they do when they're not being licked. That's like refusing to kiss someone because they threw up a week ago.

We lap up tiny amounts of piss when we suck our partners off, we swallow their spit when we kiss deeply, and we eat their shed skin cells every time we run our tongues along their bodies or nibble their sensitive bits. Having a girlfriend who menstruates means devouring trace amounts of blood and other reproductive effluvia every month, and having a boyfriend means gargling his come at regular intervals (or at least once a year on his birthday, if you're prissy). Sure, you can use barrier methods—dental dams and condoms—but for most of us, the point of oral sex is the communion you get when you take someone into your mouth. It's the trust and the wet squelchy hotness and the nastiness and the close hairy personalness of it, the tang of ball sweat and pussy stank that's unique to your own dear partner. You love them, so you love their rich gamy smells and salty tastes. They love you, so they surrender their bodies to you to be savored, trusting you not to leave visible bite marks.

When you get right down to it, we eat a lot of our partner's extrusions without giving any of it a second thought. No matter how clean we are, we're human monsters that shed copious amounts of ourselves constantly, marking our territory in shed hair and sweat and eye-gunk and the oil of our fingerprints. When we make love we end up consuming each other, wearing each other under our nails, wallowing in each other's stink like piss-soaked bed sheets. And it feels good, that's the thing, otherwise we'd all stay home and masturbate instead of trying to get it on with each other despite the inconvenience, potential for humiliation, and risk to our health. We are human animals used to pack life, not cold, solitary machines. Don't babies instinctively pop curious items into their mouths in order to learn what they are?

We mouth to gain intimate understanding of our partners. We eat to love.

I WAS USED to customers trying to buy bits of my body for their sensual delectation. Their requests rarely surprised me, though their shamelessness usually did. They'd ask for pieces of me or of my waste like restaurant-goers ordering from a menu in the blithe assumption that every aspect of my body was for sale.

Pee Guy was no big deal to me. His desire to guzzle my pee was almost flattering. Besides, it's not like I needed it—why *not* make $150 for something I was just going to flush away? *If I made $150 every time I went to the toilet,* I marveled, *I could put myself through medical school.* What I needed was a stable of pee-lovin' customers and a contract with the local spring-water delivery company. I could invest in a few glass goblets and plastic shower curtains, and I'd be good to go. Pee Guy's sessions were easy and almost festive, with his fancy glassware and his tales of European licentiousness.

Spit Guy was something else entirely. He, too, paid me good money for my precious bodily fluids, but instead of sampling my nectar from a Dixie Cup or wineglass, he liked me to hawk and spit directly into his face. I'd usually get cottonmouth halfway through our sessions and have to excuse myself to drink warm water. I charged him per session, not per spitball, since it was easier to keep track of how long I'd spent with him than to tally the times I snorted deeply, cleared my throat, and let fly.

Spit Guy begged me to hawk oysters directly into his mouth, but I drew the line at that—it was bad enough to watch him lick up my saliva secondhand without serving as both nectar *and* wineglass. Besides, I had a screaming horror of letting a big wad of spit go and having it reach his lips and tongue before it completely separated from my own mouth. If that happened, we'd be momentarily connected by a shimmering rope of saliva, and that was far too much like kissing for my taste. It was one thing to pee in a glass and watch someone drink it—that only went one way, and that direction was *away from me.* Swapping spit with a customer was a two-way street of depravity, horrible to contemplate.[1]

Though Tampon Man was never my customer, he was legendary for pushing tampons through our tip slots at the peep show. Girls doing business with Tampon Man knew to insert the

---

1. I never sold my shit to a customer. The most I did in that department was to scribble skidmarks in the cotton gusset of my panties with brown eyeliner pencil, then sell the besmirched panties to a man with a yearning for the taste of solid waste. FYI—the trick with that is to turn the panties inside out and wipe your ass with them first, so they have a realistically assy smell.

SWEET

tampons into their vaginas, then to push them back through the slot to him. He held the cotton plugs in this mouth with the strings dangling out like tea bags while he masturbated. He was cheery about his habits, rewarding his entertainers with smiles and enthusiastic thumbs-up signs when they were able to smear the tampons with actual menstrual blood. I was leery of him and his Kotex fetish. Again, watching a customer suck on my sloughed-off vaginal cells—even through glass—seemed like more genuine contact than I felt comfortable providing.

I was never asked for nail parings or dead hair—but I wouldn't put it past customers to want those things from the women they pay for erotic interaction. I've certainly sold my share of sweaty, extensively worn socks, smelly boots, and pussy-scented panties to know that pretty much anything the human body sheds naturally, *someone* will be willing to pay lots of money for. Customers want what all of us want: They crave oral communion and consumption, intimate smells, the taste of various physical nooks and crannies. They're only different in the fact that they're willing to pay a stranger for their physical relics, and that for them, the eating is enough—love never comes into play.

I'm a sentimental cannibal, though: I only eat the ones I love.

THE HUMAN BODY is a strange thing—we sweat, we fart, we blow snot, we rub deodorant under our arms to stop smells, we powder our feet, we blot our facial oil. We're so *messy*. We spend huge amounts of money on things like breath-freshening toothpaste and dandruff-control shampoo, but we know that our attempts to control our smells and secretions are essentially doomed to fail. You can scrape your gums raw with Comet and gargle with Clorox bleach every night if you want, but the next morning your tongue will be just as coated and your breath will be just as stinky. You can wipe your ass with triple-ply quilted luxury bathroom tissue that costs as much as embossed linen-weight stationery, but your shit will still make your bathroom reek like a biker bar outhouse. You can spray as much vanilla-scented air freshener as you like to cover up the shame of your successful peristalsis, but you'll just be inhaling vanilla-scented shit molecules. It's the human condition—we stink, we fuck, we eat, we shit. We're dirty animals with crusty eyes and smelly asses and rich, fruity farts that we sniff, curiously and delicately, when we're alone. We're not only filthy, we're sneaky, too: We wash our hands ostentatiously in public restrooms, then dig boogers out of our noses and wipe them on the undersides of our desks. We're all monsters.

But now my relation to the things human bodies do is different. I look at what I'm doing now—working in an office two days a week transcribing business documents where nobody knows me as a writer or a sex worker or anything other than a tired spinster with a slightly higher-than-average typing speed—versus my decade in the adult entertainment industry, and it's almost as if I've traded in one set of body things for another, entirely different one.

For the very first time in my professional life, my coworkers are unaware of whether I have pubic hair or not.

Nobody gets close enough to me to know if I've bothered to shower that morning, or if I'm showing up to work steeped in a bitter brew of last night's whiskey-sweat or covered in the light salt-crust of my boyfriend's ejaculate. My tattoos are covered, my shoes are flat and spraddling, and my body language is sedate, not sensual and beckoning. Sitting in my office chair for eight hours a day wilts my spine and flattens my ass.

In the forest of cubicles in which I now conduct my professional life, none of us ever touch. The days when I playfully slapped my coworkers' bottoms and pinched upper arms and kissed cheeks and traded makeup and drugs and food and tampons and magazines are long gone. Now when I bump into someone, I say, "Excuse me." Collisions are awkward, and we move around each other in arcs to avoid them. "Let me move," I say when a coworker needs to attend to my computer, vacating my seat and edging away miserably. There's a secret formula for how much space there must be between us all at any given time, and we all react in continual adjustment to that formula as we orbit each other in rotation between copy machine, coffee room, supply closet, and restroom. "After you," I say, holding a door and tilting my body away as much as I can to give my boss the maximum amount of passage between us. We both look away as she steps over the threshold, as if politely choosing not to mention an unpleasant odor.

I don't know my coworkers' bodies anymore. We spend hours with each other, and none of us appear to have assholes. Nobody farts, or if they do, they don't guffaw and make a proud announcement. I don't know who's on her period, or where anyone is in her cycle. I don't know who has fat knees or a bounteous ass or tight abs or bruises or scars from needle marks or surprisingly lovely, arched feet. I don't know what's beautiful about each woman now. Nobody knows what's beautiful about me. Everything human about us is deliberately hidden, tucked away, lied about, or ignored.

AGAPAE

I am desperate for scent—I track it doggedly in a vain attempt to gain olfactory information, like a truffle pig pushing its snout deep into moss. I thought I smelled someone's hair once as I stood over her, both of us peering at her monitor as she showed me a shortcut to a specific client's document template. I breathed in sharply, transfixed. It was thrillingly chemical—perhaps a dandruff shampoo like my dad used, the kind sold in blue bottles, marketed as medicine. But the excitement lay in the chase: Could I possibly smell her head sweat *underneath* the shampoo? The stink of unwashed hair is such a specific, personal scent—it's as individual as pussy odor, and I knew it, and I was suddenly inflamed, sniffing desperately, knowing I only had a few seconds before I'd have to back away to my own computer to duplicate her instruction. Then I realized I was inhaling the tiny bottle of Wite-Out that sat, opened and forgotten, on her desk.

It hadn't been her hair at all.

I never thought I'd miss the smell of Lenore's sausage-and-onion flatulence. But I do.

IN MY FLUORESCENTLY lit word-processing pit of women, surrounded like a fortress by the private offices of men, we act like none of us fuck. Like we never have, and never would, and never wanted to. We can talk about each other's children, but we can't talk about sprawling in rumpled sheets next to a loved partner, fierce and exuberant, wanting to carry his baby, to be his knocked-up bitch. We do talk about husbands, but only matter-of-factly, as if they were geriatric aunts or discreet, effeminate uncles. I don't mention my boyfriend, allowing them to assume that my nights

178

are spent alone, drinking cup after cup of herbal tea and reading starchy novels, like any other seemly old maid.

When we're forced to leave our word-processing keep to use the restroom, we scurry. We tuck our asses in and under instead of allowing them free, bouncing play. Our boobs are strapped down. And when we pass men in the common hallways we either show our teeth submissively, shucking and jiving like house servants, or we avoid eye contact and speed up, shying away from the gravitational pull of their male bodies like comets. It's as if all the fuckery has been sucked out of us, leaving us dry and sexless and efficient as smooth-crotched Barbie dolls in the elastic-waisted pantyhose that bisect our bellies in cruel red slashes. After doing our business in the ladies' room, we hurry back to our abbey breathlessly. It's better to be cloistered with the other women, safe in our cubicles, gazing into the solitary hearths of our monitors. It's less risky.

None of them know I fuck women, that I could spread their thighs and feast on their cunts like a vampire, sucking their labia into my mouth and sliding cool fingers inside them.[2] None of them know I'm hungry for the scent of their sweat, that I would lick it from their skin in salty beads if I could. It's not that I find any of them attractive—it's that in such a sterile environment, I feel rabid and feral, wild for the taste of blood, full of need and thrust and demand. I'd fuck any one of them the same way I'd bite big chunks of flesh and skin and bone from their bodies. I'd take anything I could from them that was human and febrile, warm and alive and real. I'd bite it or suck it or drink it down in

---

2. I realize as I write this that I'll need to give notice a few weeks before this book comes out.

AGAPAE

hot gushes of sluice, bending them over their desks and howling like the animal I am. I am salt and spit and come and shit and piss and blood and skin—we all are, and just once I'd like us to stop pretending to be cerebral adjuncts to our computers and admit that we're all disgusting and wonderful human monsters full of devilish desire.

I consider a fair amount of mischief, when I'm not staying home drinking herbal tea and reading novels.

I'VE SCREWED UP the eye contact thing on a number of occasions. I blame the fact that the men in the offices that surround the word-processing pit are the same ones that paid me to dance for them, dominate them, and touch their pricks for so many years. I know what these fat-bellied white men look like with the little candle-stumps of their penises in their hands. I know what they smell like when they're sitting nude on a towel, masturbating in front of a stranger posing carefully in seven-inch heels: shit and baby oil. I know the fermented-bean smell of their ball sweat. I know that they take their bloated paychecks and they spend them in dirty little shacks just outside of city limits, paying women like me to spread our pussies for them.

So it's hard for me to pretend to be flustered when they walk past me in the hallways. I've made the mistake of making eye contact, and of refusing to move aside for them, forcing them to sidestep as I pass. I've looked at them the way I've looked at my customers for a decade: evaluating them, noting what I see, then dismissing them. It's hard to take their authority seriously when I know precisely how degenerate most of them are. I know that if

I donned a padded bra and a G-string, most of these men would happily degrade themselves in my presence, rolling in their own waste and devouring their own ejaculate from shit-slicked fingers. How many men in ties have I watched jamming filthy plastic butt plugs deep into their own rectums? How many of them have implored me to beat their asses, step on their cocks, slap their faces, spit on them? How many have dribbled little yellow curds of come onto themselves in my presence? How many of them have returned to their wives afterward and made them feel unloved and unwanted, because they feel entitled to a younger stranger in Kabuki makeup by the very virtue of being able to pay for her time and brief tolerance?

So no. I guard my eyes. When I imagine whispering filth into their ears and making the equivalent of my entire paycheck for an hour's contemptuous work behind a closed office door, I distract myself. I am no longer working as an adult entertainer, I remind myself. I am a writer now. It's better now. I have more self-respect now. Don't I?

But I cannot pay my bills with what I make, and sitting still under bright lights in an office all day hurts my body and my mind grievously. I remember dancing onstage in New Orleans, flying around the pole, shaking my ass and laughing hard, kicking over drinks and plucking $20 bills from my customers' fingers like daisies. I remember the music, the nasty bass thump scooping me up and lifting me from the hips, making me feel graceful and elegant and absolutely in control, a throb radiating out from my pussy like a halo of light. I remember feeling beautiful all day long.

And I think that's what I miss the very most.

AGAPAE

THE FOOD MY office coworkers eat is mostly starch, crammed hastily into greedy mouths with keyboard-dirty fingers. They eat fast and look guilty, chewing as quickly as they can to swallow the lumps of food before anyone notices. There are many jokes about breaking diets, food going directly to hips, and "I really shouldn't, but . . . " It's like living in a Cathy cartoon. These women won't sit down and eat a piece of meat with a salad on the side, but they'll graze on Betty Crocker quick bread and grocery store bakery cake and cookies and doughnuts bought in big plastic clamshells and Halloween candy from communal bowls all day long, washed down with a slurry of bad coffee and powdered creamer.

Predictably, the only talk about our bodies as women is negative and derogatory. Our collective desire to lose weight is taken for granted. When I mention my plans to go to the gym after work, my coworkers bow their heads in penitence, saying they "should" go, but don't, and that they "need" to, because of the unmanageability of their bodies. "You're so *good*," they sigh spitefully, rolling their eyes, as if I'm some kind of apple-polishing Goody Two-Shoes accruing gold stars to their detriment. "You must be losing so much *weight*." Then they eye my body curiously. My coworkers seem confounded by my refusal to join in the general discussion of diets, "good" and "bad" foods, "problem areas" (hips, ass, thighs are the usual culprits), and by my reluctance to participate in group bingeing behavior when sugary snacks appear. Yet, I'm not thin. Why would I bother denying myself sweet treats and exercising for so little payoff?

Nobody assumes I'm going to the gym because I like going, or because after sitting trapped behind a desk for eight hours, the only thing that unkinks the muscles in my neck and shoulders and back is an hour of hot, sweaty movement. Nobody assumes I go because I love taking care of my body, or because I like being strong and flexible. To my coworkers, the gym is punishment that must be endured for the crime of eating "bad" foods, and the body is something that must be regulated and chastised, like a disobedient pet. I suspect my coworkers view themselves as essentially separate from their bodies—as if they're the superegos to their bodies' rebellious ids, as if they exist as brains and personalities living in fleshly containers that may or may not be to their liking, like gamers developing rich, complex online existences and referring contemptuously to "meat space." But after ten years of living in my body as a performer, a dancer, and a model, I can't make that division. I *am* my body. My body is me. We're all on the same team—brain, heart, muscles, everything. And my team doesn't like nasty grocery store bakery cakes or flaccid, underdone spice cakes or cookies that taste of grease and corn syrup and salt. So I don't eat them.

My coworkers have no idea that I made a good income for a decade portraying sexiness and erotic availability. Like most women who have never worked in the sex industry, my coworkers assume men fantasize about Victoria's Secret models and other instances of corporeal freakishness held up as praised examples by the three-headed media/fashion/diet industry Cerberus, because advertisers make more money from us when we're miserable.

But if there's anything I learned from my customers, it's that when folks pay for sexual entertainment, they want a woman who loves her own body, first and foremost. They'd rather jerk off to an average girl in a great costume who radiates pride and confidence than they would a supermodel, and for all the oppressiveness of the sex industry, the one thing you can't accuse it of is elitism. The adult industry tells a lot of unforgivably ugly lies about women, female desire, and erotic love in general, but it also taught me to walk with my back straight and my head up. My big ass and thick thighs paid my rent for a score of years—not because I was ashamed of them, but because I brazenly displayed them. And of course I wasn't to every customer's taste—but that's where the egalitarianism of the industry comes in, because every girl is going to be attractive to a certain population of buyers if she simply allows them to admire her and reinforces that desire by demonstrating her own belief in herself. In such a massive industry, there's room for a wide variety of entrepreneurial gumption.

It also helps if you're willing to sell your pee and your saliva. I'm not saying the industry isn't disgusting—I'm saying it's *equally* disgusting, that it's an Equal Opportunity Employer of filth. I'm saying if you *want* to pee in a wineglass for rent money, you pretty much can, as long as you value yourself enough to drive a hard bargain for your golden nectar. And parenthetically, I find peeing in a glass for $150 much less degrading than working for minimum wage. I'd rather serve someone a piping hot glass of urine for a fee I've negotiated on my own behalf than a double grande caramel mochaccino with whipped cream for an employer who holds me in utter contempt and pays me just enough to stay exhausted, overworked, and demoralized.

I'm fully aware of the absurdity of having learned to love my body by working in such a legendarily woman-hating industry. I hate that I had to show my tits in order to learn to love them, that slapping a price tag on my pussy taught me to respect my own physical value, not only as a female, but as a living, breathing human being worthy of nourishing food, loving care, and respect. It's a damn paradox, and I feel like I'm skating dangerously close to the kind of bullshit pro-adult-industry "sex positive" *rah-rah*ism I despise. So I want to say this again: The sex industry is mostly very, very fucked up. It pushes us apart from each other and teaches us to use each other as objects, instead of seeing each other as real, living, complicated human beings. But it's also got little islands of okay-ness in the midst of all its horrible, alienating lies—and one of them is that it's hard to hate your own body when it has become your best friend and strongest ally in your pursuit of a livable wage. When even your waste is valuable, you're forced to acknowledge—and respect—your own inherent physical worth.

You have to take wisdom where you can find it. Wouldn't it be ideal if we learned to love our bodies as children and grew up with unshakable inner confidence impervious to even the canniest advertisers' lies? What if we didn't have to whore our bodies to discover their value? What if we just *knew* our bodies deserved love and care? What if we woke up feeling beautiful and treated ourselves like beautiful creatures all day long and woke up the next morning and did it again? How would our lives be different?

I'm guessing we'd eat a lot less store-bought junk food. And that far fewer of us would choose to tolerate the insidious torture of a forty-hour workweek spent, cramped and aching, behind a desk.

TRICK

TWO DAYS BEFORE HALLOWEEN, MY OFFICE MANAGER TOLD me that we—the entire word-processing department—were expected to dress up in costume for the office holiday party.

"The clients enjoy it so much," she trilled. "It's fun and festive!"

From 3:00 to 5:00 PM, I was informed, my department would be mingling with our clients in a big conference room, cheerfully entertaining them as costumed team players rife with holiday spirit. I imagined cotton-picking Negroes singing spirituals for their indulgent masters. *Festive* wasn't the word I would have chosen, but it was clear I would need to drum up a nonoffensive, work-safe costume anyway. Two hours of standing and walking instead of being crouched behind my desk sounded like heavenly reprieve, even if I'd have to do it in a conference room filled with the men whose letters I typed.

According to my enthusiastic manager, some of the clients also dressed up for the annual bash. I was looking forward to the probability of seeing a few of the old white men who made up our client base in garish makeup and pantyhose—that old balloon-titted dude-in-a-dress routine never seems to go out of fashion for conservative guys looking for a reliably "outrageous" Halloween costume. Most straight men who dress as women for comedic effect botch their drag deliberately—walking flat-footed and exposing thick mats of hair at their décolleté—as if to underscore their own masculinity the way a lovely woman in a tailored suit can appear even more feminine and fragile than one in a dress. Unlike drag queens, though, their aggressive desire for the trappings of femininity has always seemed less like tribute and more like invasion, as if they're daring us to ban them from any area of our lives, including the most intimate details of our own adornment.

But due to my previous work as a fetish-oriented dominatrix, I couldn't help wondering how many of our cross-dressed clients would enjoy wearing their costume garb later—for erotic purposes—once the Halloween festivities were over. How many straight men had perched in front of my prop vanity table, jiggling their bare legs impatiently as I applied lipstick to the mouths that barked orders all day? How many had confessed the simple desire to be "pretty," then in the same breath to be "treated like a slut"? My cross-dressing salarymen spent their days delegating their workload to women making $10 an hour, then they paid strangers a couple hundred bucks to watch them jerk off into a pair of panties. Men like them were far from uncommon—I could shave a rich old man's legs with a disposable razor faster than I could shave my own.

Which meant I had a good chance of spotting a cross-dressed executive at the office Halloween party—the type who was just a little bit too serious about his makeover routine, or slightly too graceful in his high heels. Someone who didn't just dress up in an evening gown once a year for yuks—a man who regularly stole and wore his wife's lingerie under his business suits, or who paid a stranger like me to dress him up in satin and lace, paint his nails, then bully him into orgasm. Spotting him would mean knowing I could make the equivalent of my paycheck behind his closed office door by whispering ridiculous filth like "You little slut—I'll bet your naughty pussy is wet," into his ear, or by making him wear my panties as he typed his own damn correspondence.

Not that I *would*. Not anymore, anyway. But those old instincts die hard.

IT WAS SO easy back then. It was like making money by breathing. The best part was, they didn't even care how sexy I was because their whole focus was on how sexy *they* were. *They* were the hot ones, *they* were the whores—but only a fool would think that a female dominant is somehow turning the tables on her customers or "transgressing gender roles" by treating her customers like sluts. All that kind of verbal play does is confirm their belief that it's right and natural for real women to be treated similarly in the cosmology of porn—i.e., sluts wear lingerie and should be punished for their whorish nature by forced sexual performance,

SWEET

which they invariably enjoy. That's not a message I've ever felt good about spreading. Eventually my reluctance to work in a system predicated on human objectification drove me out of the adult industry entirely.

But the money—Lord, how I missed the money! Fifteen minutes of watching a fat man rub himself through a lace thong, stockings pulled up to his knees, occasionally prodding his chest with the end of my riding crop and calling him a wet-pussied bitch—and oh, how the money rolled in. And oh, how I spent it: restaurant meals, travel, clothes, taxis, the best liquor, the purest drugs. I spent thoughtlessly—money flowed through me. It seemed like there would always be more of it, as if I could just reach out when I wanted more and scoop it up, like a bear lazily pawing salmon from a jumping creek.

It wasn't out of the realm of possibility that some of the office's clients had actually been my customers in the past. Seattle's a small town, and there are relatively few places for men to go where they can engage in gray-area, semi-legal sexual activity with paid professionals. I was almost positive I'd recognize some of them if they had their cocks out. I wasn't much for remembering faces, but every cock has its own quirks.

FIND H'WEEN COSTUME, I scrawled on a Post-it note to myself after my boss returned to her cubicle. I had two days. I knew I could think of something. Maybe I'd shove a balloon in my pants and go in costume as a sexualized, clownish man, to give any cross-dressed clients a taste of their own medicine.

I imagined myself at the office party, rubbing my balloon

cock between a bewigged and heavily made-up client's balloon tits. "Take it, bitch," I'd say. The squeak of latex would be the only response. I could drizzle ranch dressing from the inevitable supermarket crudités platter over his balloons as I "finished." *See how you* really *like being treated like a slut*, I imagined myself saying.

My business-casual slacks didn't have pockets—to reduce the theft of pens and other office supplies, I supposed—so I jammed the Post-it note into the handbag that sat under my desk next to my recycling bin and wastebasket. After a moment, I tossed the entire pad of Post-it notes into my purse, then added a stapler and a spool of cellophane tape. Maybe instead of going to the party as a balloon-cocked stud, I'd go as a white-collar criminal. I wouldn't even have to buy a costume—I'd just carry all the office supplies I'd stolen over the last six months in a big paper grocery sack.

AT HOME, I STARED AT THE CLOTHES IN MY CLOSET, TROLLING for costume ideas. All my clothes were limp and black—if I wanted to dress up as an Amish person or someone with schizotypal personality disorder, I was good to go. Other than that, I was without inspiration.

I considered purchasing a premade costume at the Halloween store down the street, but I wanted to avoid wearing anything "sexy" and most of their offerings for women were short, tight, and made of PVC. I hated "sexy" Halloween costumes, especially the kind from companies that made most of their money selling plastic dresses to non-sex-working ladies trying to be risqué. I knew some people found it exciting to dress up like whorish versions of working-class women—the perennial popularity of the French maid costume is proof enough of that—but as a working-class woman who's actually whored, the last thing I wanted to do was wear a cheaply made snap-front dress that reminded me of my previous incarnation. I had no desire to have my cleavage gazed at by the clients who currently paid my tiny salary when I used to make so much more from executives exactly like them without typing a single letter.

I may be a faded office flower, I thought, *but I'm no fool.*

And besides—the old white men in evening gowns, heels, and wigs would be plenty "sexy" enough.

AS I PONDERED balloon cocks and non-"sexy" costumes, I realized the answer was hanging right in my face. I laughed incredulously as I reached out and petted my tightest, oldest, most beat-up pair of Levi's, which hung in the shadow of all the black clothing in my closet.

Tight, pegged boy-pants—my motorcycle boots—a concert T-shirt. I'd add plenty of metal-studded belts around my waist and cuffs on my wrists, and a handkerchief folded flat and tied around my head. Underneath my bandanna, my hair would be matted, teased, and sprayed. I'd show my tattoos and wear black eyeliner. The pièce de résistance would be Beau's biker jacket. And voilà—I'd be Axl Rose, Rock Star Royalty, life-size and in full color, like a glossy page ripped out of *Rolling Stone* and shoved in everyone's face.

I pulled my Levi's off their hanger and began rooting through my concert T-shirts for the most beat-up, bleach-stained, hole-y specimen.

As I assembled my costume, I had to admit that I especially loved the idea of showing my ink as Axl, since I'd been hiding my tattoos since the day the Xeroxed dress code had appeared in my inbox after I'd had the poor judgment to push up my sleeves one hot and busy afternoon. I looked forward to parading my Technicolor skin around like a banner of defiance for a day, just to bring a little *Appetite for Destruction* to their stultifying office world. They couldn't make me cover it up if it was part of my costume, could they?

I'm Axl fucking Rose, bitch.

THERE'S A REASON ROCK star boys have been reinterpreting the same general look for decades. It just *works*. It's sweet, and hot. It says, "I'm an asshole," "I have a big dick," and possibly, dangerously, "I use drugs." And to most of us ladies, the combination of two or three of those qualities is catnip. It's irresistible. We want to roll in that rock star/asshole quality, inhale it, and take it inside us. We *need* it. It makes us wet, and hard. It makes us *hungry*. And whether that's to fuck the nasty long-haired boy in the motorcycle boots with the Fu Manchu mustache, or to *be* him—well, what's the difference, really?

All I knew is that if I couldn't actually *be* Axl Rose circa 1987, when he was riding the crest of the killer typhoon soon to be known to the entire rockin' world as Guns N' Roses—well, at least I could dress like him one day out of the year.

Two days later, and despite my previous reservations, I attended my first office Halloween party in a sexy costume after all.

It was the kind of sexy that lived in my pussy and lower gut, more about the hot thrum I felt inside than the way I looked on the outside. My tattoos were out in all their heavy metal glory, skulls and flowers twisting up my arms like vines. I wore a sports-bra that packed my tits back against my chest but I couldn't help the way my hips swung, loose and saucy, as I clumped into the conference room in my heavy, chain-wrapped boots. I didn't stuff an actual phallus in my britches made from a sock and a condom, the way Mick taught me. Dressing like a boy was one thing, but I was scared I'd be sent home for harboring such an untoward bulge.

But even without a Little Axl filling out my Levi's, I felt like a stallion. With my tight boy-pants slung around my hips I was a strutting, preening rock star, cock-centric and insatiable; just waiting for my next sloppy blow job. I felt predatory in a way I thought I'd left behind when I traded my stiletto-heeled boots for sensible slacks, swapping the power to negotiate my own fees and determine my own labor conditions for an hourly wage and a bunch of purloined office supplies.

IF I EVER decide to get back into business, I now know which executive on my floor is the covert cross-dresser.

There were a few dudes in dresses at the party as predicted—a Raggedy Ann, a Marilyn Monroe with a virile beard, a Dorothy in a gingham dress and red Converse high-tops—but only one cross-dressed fellow was attempting to hide an erection between his own thighs. Although I didn't recognize him as a past client, I knew him for what he was. He wore an Elvira costume, his thin lips smeared with his wife's expensive department store lipstick, cutting our store-bought sheet cake with shaky, excited hands.

Hello, you wet-pussied little bitch, I thought as I stared into his face.

He blushed as he handed me a paper plate full of cake.

Not that I'd ever say anything like that for real. Those days are over. I work as a typist in an office now, not as a dominatrix in a dungeon, and for the most part, I harbor little regret. Morally, I made the only choice I could.

But old instincts die hard.

TREAT

I HAVE A BAG OF FUN-SIZE REESE'S PEANUT BUTTER CUPS
in my cupboard. It's nearly Halloween, so I'm allowed. I'm also
allowed every other day of the year because I'm a grownup, and
if I want to have ten fun-size pieces of candy for dinner I can. In
that respect (and ignoring the twin bummers of paying rent and
going to work), adulthood is every bit as fabulous as I thought it
would be when I was a little girl, forced to eat well-balanced nutritious meals by my hippie parents. They meant well but didn't
realize their insistence on fruits, whole grains, and vegetables
would result in a maturity spent dining on convenience store
fare. Every time I bite into a Twinkie I am profoundly grateful that it is not a carrot stick, and I see no reason why a pack
of Oberto Cocktail Pep can't be just as nutritive as a boneless,

skinless chicken breast. If you take a multivitamin with the pepperoni, what's the difference, really?

Fun-size Reese's Peanut Butter Cups are smaller now than they used to be when I was a child wistfully cruising the grocery store candy aisle in the weeks leading up to Halloween. Some howling demon at Hershey's decided that a smaller peanut butter cup would be more "fun." I don't get it: We're fatter than ever. So why would we want a *smaller* peanut butter cup? Shouldn't candy manufacturers be concentrating on making their products bigger, to supply our increasing sugar-jones? Or are the individual pieces of candy getting smaller with the understanding that their reduced size gives us tacit permission to eat many more pieces than we ordinarily would?

"Fun-size," my big white ass. A Reese's Peanut Butter Cup the size of a throw pillow—now *that* would be fun.

And best of all, I'm pretty sure one would be enough.

SWEET

Fried Chicken
Interlude:
Chicken Bus

☠

ON THE BUS COMING HOME FROM WORK ONE NIGHT, a homeless man threw a piece of Dumpster chicken at me.

I hurled it back at him and the chicken hit him in the face, hard. It bounced into his lap, leaving a greasy smear on his pants before falling to the floor. The chicken looked like it might have been good about two days ago.

"What's wrong with you, you rude motherfucker?" I snarled.

He smiled, his mouth full of mashed-up chicken and homeless spit.

"I'm a nigger!" he said.

Under the layers of worn-in grime on his face, he was as white as I was.

"No, you're not!" I said, indignant. "You're just a rude, homeless, chicken-throwing piece of shit!"

An actual black man was sitting across the aisle from me. I hoped he didn't think I thought *nigger* was a normal word to say.

The homeless dude and I stared at each other.

"Get the fuck off this bus," I said.

"This ain't your bus, bitch," the homeless man pointed out. He swallowed the chewed-up chicken-wad in one gulp. I saw the mass of old smelly chicken travel down his throat and disappear into the collar of his filthy overcoat.

"It's my bus now, cocksucker," I said, then mentally slapped my own forehead. That's the thing about shit-talking: You have to back your words up and even fight for them no matter how dumb or improbable they are, so when you're bumping chests with an opponent, you really have to watch what you say. Now I'd moved the point of contention from him pegging me with fried chicken—justified—to my claim of bus ownership—totally unjustified. I was willing to spar over my right not to be hit with rotten chicken, but backing up my hasty delineation of territory was going to be tricky.

The black guy got up briskly and moved a few seats away from us. I didn't blame him. Now I was going to have to fight a homeless chicken-fingered lunatic for bus ownership because I said I owned it and I had to back myself. I didn't relish the thought. I wished I'd stuck with the chicken as the issue, or maybe his use of the word *nigger*. Either one of those things would have been better than fighting over who was the ruler of the bus.

After a moment, the homeless man slung another piece of chicken toward the driver at the front of the bus. It was a more casual toss, like he was just checking out the idea of slinging chicken at someone other than me.

FRIED CHICKEN INTERLUDE

The driver pulled our bus—*my* bus—over. "Get off!" the driver ordered over the crackly bus speaker.

The homeless man crammed a slimy chicken breast into his mouth, carrying it sideways like a hunting dog retrieving a duck. He muttered around the piece of chicken, but I couldn't understand what he was saying. A delicate string of drool worked its way around the chicken and touched the lapel of his overcoat. Finally, he chucked a wing at the driver—more decisively this time, as if he'd made a decision and was sticking to it—and exited the bus through the back doors. The drivers aren't supposed to open the back doors after 7:00 PM, but perhaps special circumstances like having chicken tossed at you call for amendments to the rules.

As I got off, I thanked the driver for throwing the homeless chicken-tossing dude off the bus.

"Yeah," the driver said wearily. The whole front of the bus smelled like rotten chicken.

I wondered how much longer he had to drive.

On my way home, I stopped at KFC for a bucket of the Colonel's Original Recipe. Gnawing on a drumstick at the bus stop, I glared defiantly at the people passing me on the sidewalk. I had ammunition, a getaway bus due in seven minutes, and two lemon-scented wet-wipes. The next person who threw anything at me, said the word *nigger*, or showed me a mouth full of chewed-up chow was getting it with both finger-lickin' barrels.

IV.
PAIN

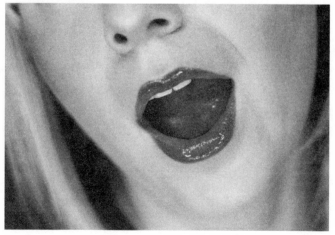

INTRODUCTION

MY DEAR FRIEND MARIA CAUTIONED ME ABOUT WRITING THIS BOOK.

"Writing a book about something you *were*—or something you *did*—is easy," she said, in the sweet North Carolina burr that tucks in the ends of words neatly but allows their vowels free, bewildering play. "That's just *history*. But writing a book about something you *are* is hard, because that's gonna keep changing."

She's a wise owl, that Maria. And oh man, was she right.

It turns out that writing about something you *are* is pretty much a losing proposition. The very process of documenting your current state of mind is guaranteed to change that state of mind, no matter how fast you scribble stuff down. When you go back and reread something that felt achingly true a week ago, more often than not you end up hating yourself, because what was true then is not true now, and the conclusions you drew proudly at the time now seem worse than fatuous. You can edit, of course, but it's not like your edits are going to pin down the truth any more effectively than your first draft did. Rewriting is just substituting a slightly more current edition of the truth, which—in another week—will be equally outdated.

Essentially, you're fucked from the git-go. You go into battle boldly, accompanied by a great deal of fanfare, waving a big white banner that reads TRUTH, like you're the first person in the world brave enough to tell the real, true story of whatever it is you're writing about—and by the end of your book your banner has turned to muddy ribbons that you're constantly stumbling over and cursing, and at a certain point you make a deal with yourself that if you can just get the damn thing finished, you'll never be dumb enough to charge into the fray again.

This is why writers are legendary drunks, by the way. We sit at home raking through our own shit for little knots of usable nutrition, which we pop back into our mouths and chew hopefully. We're the filtration system for our own words. At the end of the process, all the tiny lumps of matter that survive end up being pruned and polished into a publishable manuscript by our editors, while we strain to expel the sickening bloat of all the waste-words we've gobbled, wiping our poor asses raw with the shreds of our TRUTH banners. Writing a book is not an occupation that offers much dignity. It's like shitting in county lockup: Everyone has to smell the curdled remains of what you ate the day before, and, if you're lucky, they won't shank you for it.

HALFWAY THROUGH THE year it took me to write this book, I became severely depressed. I was broke, with no way to pay my rent or to buy groceries, and I was too sick to work. With no insurance, I was unable to afford hospitalization or close medical supervision, so I spent my days on the Internet, researching firearms. I called my friends in the medical field for advice on where to place the barrel of the gun. "It's research for my book," I told them, though I hadn't written a word in months. I stopped showering—what was the point? Eventually, I stopped leaving the apartment. Garbage piled up and stank. I didn't care.

My depression stopped this book cold.

Then, my laptop contracted a massive virus. My operating system had to be wiped clean and reinstalled. I lost thousands of MP3s—nearly my entire song library. In a stroke of unbelievable luck, my notes for this book were salvaged by a data-retrieval specialist, as was the existing draft manuscript. Despite that, I began to exhibit all the posttraumatic stress syndromes I'd experienced after Hurricane Katrina: nightmares, insomnia, constant trembling, random public weeping, the whole anxiety suite. My body weight plummeted and my blood pressure shot up like a paper snake.

Then my partner and I broke up. Got back together. Broke up again.

My suicidal ideation got focused and specific. A Pacific Northwest girl to the core, I decided to pull a Kurt Cobain: I'd overdose on heroin, then blow my head off with a shotgun. I didn't plan on leaving a note—that was just more writing I couldn't do, one more missed deadline.

I figured I'd wait until after the winter holidays so I didn't ruin anyone's Christmas.

SO, PAIN. I know from pain. Most of this book was brought forth in pain, and at this point I think pain is just as much a part of the writing process as actually pushing the words out and smearing them around. I've never experienced childbirth, but it seems right to me that bringing forth new life should cause agony—otherwise, every simpleton would write symphonies and we'd all have a dozen vanity babies to feed. At this point I think the purpose of the pain is transformative—it burns away the nonessential stuff, strips us bare, and forces us to give up the goods long after we've stopped caring about anything but finding a way to end our anguish.

My depression waned when I found a physician willing to see me for $10 a visit on an under-the-table sliding scale that probably saved my life. I started taking the medication she prescribed, and two weeks later I noticed that I was showering and leaving the house again. Now I take pills three times a day, and every time I do I am grateful to a physician who put healing above self-interest and to a therapist who held me tight and wouldn't let me fall.

"FUGU" AND "WASABI" are two short pieces about food as danger. I'm positive I'm not the only person who likes the occasional culinary belt across the mouth—sometimes you need your food to show you who's boss.

"Boundary Issues" reveals the one substance I won't put in my mouth.

"Loaves and Fishes" is a cheery little piece about the lighter side of chronic poverty.

And "Heartbreak" is about staying alive.

Pour yourself a glass of whiskey, and let's get down to business.

INTRODUCTION

FUGU

SOME FOODS ARE BAD FOR YOU. THEY WILL HURT YOU IF you eat them, but you eat them anyway.

You know this when you're little—the knowledge seeps into your bones, jacketed in more general parental warnings about Bad Dogs and Strangers In Cars Offering Rides.

Halloween candy can hurt you when it is offered—blatantly unwrapped, or with their plastic wrappings mysteriously loose— at the door of a house full of bleary-eyed hippies who don't seem to understand that you're in costume. To them, "Trick or Treat!" means *Give me several small boxes of raisins that I will discard immediately upon returning home.*

Apples—similarly shoved into pillowcases on Halloween night—are also very dangerous. They usually contain razor blades, placed there by fiends who joyfully anticipate the suffering of local legions of small children with slashed gums. If you receive an apple for Halloween you must take it to your local police precinct, where it will be x-rayed. This is for your safety.

If you're lactose-intolerant, you're probably familiar with searing self-recrimination. You casually drink a glass of milk or have a bowl of ice cream, and an hour later you're squatting on the toilet cradling your lower belly or—worse—passing painful, noxious clouds of gas that alienate you from even the most tolerant of your friends and coworkers, including the vegan ones accustomed to their own massive, fibrous vegi-farts.

The worst part is, *you know this*. It's not the pain that wounds—it's the knowledge that the pain could have been avoided, that you basically ushered Pain in, made it a drink, fluffed its pillows, and made it feel welcome. Your greed opened the door and Pain came in, swirling its cape like a vampire, baring pointed little teeth. It just had to be invited.

SOME FOODS AREN'T even foods, but we eat them anyway. Then when we get sick from them, we wonder why we even bothered to attempt to gain nourishment from something that was so clearly a bad idea. Splenda goes into this category. As does that supposed scientific breakthrough from a few years ago, low-calorie *fake fat*, made of microscopically tiny beads that loll on your tongue and give your poor, tricked mouth the sensation of luxury and rich, smooth abundance. Of course later in your GI tract the little fake-fat beads continue to slide and roll, resulting in wet, blatting farts and shit-stained pants.

Fake fat, the industrial food conglomerates trumpeted—*the choice of a new generation!* (A generation that, presumably, smells suspiciously of liquid shit. No matter, though, as long as the shit is decorating the crotch and rear of fabulously skinny, size 6 jeans.)

Frankly, just eat the whole bag of normal chips. They may make you chunky if you eat them often, and they sure as hell won't do your heart any favors, but at least chips made with regular fat won't blow through the gutter of your intestines like wet mud an hour after you devour them, after guiltily licking the salt-crumbs from your fingers in an attempt to wring flavor out of desiccated potato-sheaves dipped in tiny beads of plastic.

Have the real ones. Really.

SOME FOODS WILL hurt you, all right. Some can kill you.

We love consuming danger—putting it in our mouths, sucking on it, rolling it around on our tongues. There's a reason sushi made with fugu is expensive, delectable, hard to find, exciting: Blowfish is riddled with poison, and only the most cunning chef can slip the poison away from the meat with the tip of his knife without the flesh becoming infected. Even so, fugu buzzes on the tongue, numbing the palate with tiny, homeopathic doses of death.

Supposedly—and I've never had any—but supposedly, fugu sushi is a rush. It gets you high. You eat it and become breathless and giggly. It feels good—the expense is worth it. It's an experience like no other—the culinary equivalent of Russian roulette. Is your chef deft enough to have prepared your fish correctly? You can't know until you eat it, and either live—your lips and tongue stinging with pleasure—or die, asphyxiating on the floor of a Japanese restaurant with paper chopstick wrappers in your hair.

All the risk of death makes the ecstasy of continuing to live that much more piquant. You leave the restaurant, safe and full of raw protein and *alive,* and it's as if you've been given a second chance, directly from the hand of God. He kept you alive, didn't He? All Appalachian Christian snake-handling/glass-eating cult members know that when you give your life to God, He can choose to keep you alive or not and if He does, it's for a reason. The reason is, you're righteous. It's not luck. It's glory.

Oh, and it's illegal in the United States, so finding a chef willing to serve it to you is like doing a drug deal.

It is worth it. I've been assured of that by an adventurous friend curious enough about what it feels like to almost, nearly, not-quite die, to go through the laborious process of tracking fugu down. He paid for it with cash, just in case—like any other illegal transaction, like buying heroin or a woman's body. And he ate it with rice and soy sauce, I imagine, and tiny green blobs of *wasabi* to enhance . . . whatever flavor fugu actually possesses. The flavor wasn't notable enough to warrant mention, but my friend took almost half an hour to describe the details of the "buy" in salacious, chops-licking detail.

"Would you eat it again?" I asked him. And, "Did it get you high?"

"Oh yeah, I'd totally eat it again!" he said. And, "Oh yeah, I was fucking *flying.*"

We consume danger, and by eating it we conquer it, and it nourishes us. Death becomes life inside our bodies in a transubstantiation that is mystical, indescribable, exalting.

The flavor of fugu—like the taste of gun oil on the barrel of the shotgun lodged against our palates, or the vinegar-and-brown-sugar scent of the black tar we slide into the soft bend of our inner elbows—the flavor is, of course, beside the point.

My friend was right in not mentioning it. It was beneath mention. The deliciousness of fugu doesn't live in its flavor.

Or, maybe it would be more precise to say that the only important thing to mention about the flavor of fugu is that it tastes very, very dangerous. That I can know for sure, without even tasting it.

PAIN

WASABI

BEAU HAD A CANKER SORE, SO I LICKED MY FINGER AND poked it into a box of baking soda. Then I pulled his lip down and patted the soda into his sore with my fingertip.

"How does it feel?" I asked.

"It burns," he winced. I resisted the sudden desire to suck on his lower lip. It was so full and juicy I wanted to squirt yellow mustard on it and bite into it like a Ball Park frank. I loved Beau's mouth. I wanted it to feel better so he could put his mouth on my pussy again. It had been days and I was getting squirrelly.

"That's okay. Just wait, and it'll start feeling better," I said. Baking soda is basic, in terms of pH—and canker sores are usually caused by too much acidity in the mouth. Putting baking soda on a canker sore helps neutralize the pH, so your mouth can heal.

I added, "If you have a Coke, be sure to rinse your mouth out with water afterward. It's acidic *and* sugary."

Beau looked at me trustingly. He didn't know that I'd just been fantasizing about forcing his face between my legs and making him suck me until I howled. And I didn't really want to hurt him. It's just that my desire was so honed, so sharp.

I gave him a single solicitous kiss on the cheek instead.

THERE'S A WHOLE category of food that gives us the *Venus in Furs* treatment—it wounds us grievously, then it turns right around and makes us feel better than we ever knew we could feel. When it wants to, cruel food can be mind-blowingly savory, the kind of food you'd do just about anything to experience again. That's when it's not making us wish we'd never tasted it in the first place.

AN OLD BOYFRIEND told me a story about wasabi—the pistachio-green horseradish paste served with pickled ginger in sushi restaurants. The first time he went out for sushi, he assumed the blob of green stuff on his plate was a smear of avocado.

Oh, cool, he thought. *Fusion cuisine!* (This wasn't his fault. He was from California.)

Accordingly, he scooped up the entire blob of wasabi and spread it across one piece of tuna *hosomaki.*

His friend thought he was joking. "Dude . . . do you know what that is?"

"Of course I do," said my ex-boyfriend, ever the culinary sophisticate. "It's like guaca—" And then, of course, his mouth was

PAIN

exploding in a five-alarm Chicago fire of hot mustardy pain, and his eyes were squeezed shut and oozing tears, and his friend was both laughing and trying to give him his glass of water, which only made the burning feel worse.[1]

My ex got a whopping dose of gastronomic domination that day. His experience was humiliating and painful, and, what's more, it seemed to come out of nowhere, like a run of bad luck. But afterward, the endorphin rush made him feel light-headed, a little silly. The cool fish felt exquisite on his hot, irritated tongue. The sushi he ate that day was a delectable revelation.

And like anyone else given the same treatment by the same Mistress, he came creeping back for more a few days later—shame-faced, hopeful, with his money clutched in his hand.

He went back to the same restaurant, alone. He ordered himself a platter of tuna and salmon and eel and shrimp, ignoring the smirking sushi chefs behind the tall counter in the back of the restaurant. When his order arrived (along with a glass of ice water pointedly delivered by the giggling waitress), he used the tip of his chopstick to apply a minute, DNA-evidence amount of wasabi to each bite, so sheer that it didn't even look green atop his rice and fish.

But he knew it was there, and, better yet, he'd learned respect. He'd learned to play by the rules. He wasn't in charge. The terms of the exchange were dictated to him. And, like a sudden

---

1. When you eat something that's too hot, don't reach for water. Reach for something bland and starchy, like plain rice or a small piece of bread—something that will absorb the heat instead of simply spreading it through your mouth more effectively. Think of a stove-top fire: The last thing you do is throw water on it. Just put a metal or glass mixing bowl over it. You have to throttle a grease fire, not drown it.

WASABI

slap in the face followed by a loving caress, the pain he sought was directly, inextricably connected to his pleasure.

He feasted, enthralled.

E.T.: THE EXTRA-TERRESTRIAL made me cry like a little bitch, and it wasn't because I didn't know what was coming when those government men in the white zip-up suits showed up. No, I knew *exactly* what was going to go down. Did that stop me from whimpering into my Jujubes half an hour later when E.T. was pale and sick and wanting to go home? No, siree. When he poked his light-up finger at his heart during his big goodbye scene with Elliott and said "Ouch," I bawled like I was getting my leg sawed off, even though even the littlest kids in the movie theater knew he was going to rig a way to go home from bicycle parts and an old record player. We all knew, and we all cried anyway.

You can know exactly how something works, but that knowledge won't make you immune from its effects. On the contrary: We tend to enjoy provoking ourselves into physical reaction, whether we're jerking off to porn or paying to cry while E.T. flies home.

We're crack-monkeys: Once we figure out how to manipulate our own feelings, we'll hit the same button over and over again for the sheer joy of being able to create our own emotional reality.

Similarly, once you figure out that the burn of wasabi is an inseparable part of your enjoyment of it, you start playing with that burn. Yearning for it. Seeing how much you can take. You plan for it, and in some cases, you budget for it. No price is too high for that kind of teetering ecstasy—being strung up between the poles of torment and tranquility, between agony and bliss. A bland diet stultifies. Exquisitely keen sensation smacks us on the ass, wakes us up, resets our focus.

Five Stars in a Thai restaurant.

Hot peppers—the little, mean ones.

Chinese mustard.

Horseradish.

Half a bottle of hot sauce dumped over your scrambled eggs first thing in the morning.

The venomous slow burn of an Indian curry.

The list is endless, but they're all imperious divas that torment us with our own desire. They hurt us intimately, inside our bodies, and we simply can't get enough of it. At first we appreciate the pain for being the harbinger of our pleasure. Soon we learn to love the pain itself, *for* itself. We love the chemicals it releases in our brains, and we love the way it makes us sweat. We love testing our own limits, competing against ourselves. When you start to notice the ecstatic expressions on the faces of the participants as the burn brings the rush, hot-chili-eating contests become pornographic. They're gorging on pain right in front of us.

We truly are asking for it.

Spicy food makes masochists of us all.

BOUNDARY ISSUES

I'VE DINED ON A SLEW OF ROBUSTLY WEIRD ITEMS—INNARDS, pig's feet, deep-fried Mars Bars, and Mexican cake frosting made of equal parts granulated sugar, food coloring, and lard, notably. But what I won't even try, what is completely nonnegotiable to me, is cheese.

Yes, cheese. Unforgivable for a *bonne vivante*, I know. I should love it—it's creamy, generally high in fat, and uniquely flavorful— all shared attributes of other foods I adore. It's expensive. It's a luxury. It's a *treat*. People show off their fancy cheese knowledge the way others like to display their erudite taste in wine. In fact, I have a dear friend in San Francisco who's writing an entire book on cheese, and it's a testament to his talent that I look forward to reading his book despite its subject matter. I'll read it, sure, but

I won't have any idea of the tastes and textures he's describing. Because frankly, cheese makes me puke.

With two exceptions. My cheese-phobia has an Italian food clause: I'll eat mozzarella on pizza, and I'll shake Kraft parmesan from the big green can in my refrigerator onto my spaghetti when I'm feeling daring. My suspicion is that if you cover *anything* with enough garlic and oregano, even cheese, it becomes magically delicious. I'd cheerfully devour a live rat if it were dredged in Italian-seasoned breadcrumbs and fried in olive oil with plenty of minced garlic.

But bleu, cheddar, cream, brie, swiss, feta? Gouda, chevre, fontina, cottage? Camembert, provolone, paneer, havarti, muenster, limburger? No—a thousand times no. *No*, as in I won't even try it. *No*, as in I won't eat a dish that contains even trace amounts. I'll put a lot of things in my mouth, it's true, but I draw the line at cheese. That's a hard boundary, and I'm not afraid to safe-word.

In a lifetime of gleeful eating, I've only been cheese-raped twice. Once was a mistake, and the other occurred with only the best of intentions. These two incidents not only confirmed my cheese hatred but upped the ante, turning cheese from something I don't eat by choice into something I cannot contemplate eating without breathing deliberately to avoid retching. The echo chamber of early trauma is a gift that keeps on giving, amplifying itself through memory.

The mistake occurred when I was nineteen years old. I was waiting tables in a small restaurant ten blocks from my childhood home. Each server could order a shift meal—anything we liked, as long as it didn't include meat or fish or anything else deemed too expensive to be poured into our common trough as slop. For my shift meal, I was in the habit of requesting a green salad, which could be tossed with one of three dressings: balsamic vinaigrette, ranch, or bleu cheese. I always specified balsamic vinaigrette and begged for a few contraband strips of grilled chicken. Sometimes I got them, other times I didn't—my access to protein depended on the cook's mood. He usually added fat slices of preserved beets, though, which he knew I loved.

One day the line cook, flustered by a flurry of unaccountable midafternoon lunch orders, delivered my special salad dressed with bleu cheese instead of vinaigrette. Had I realized his mistake, as hungry as I was, I would have simply thrown the salad out, chicken strips and all. But I was busy bringing drinks to new tables and I didn't inspect my meal carefully, and on my way to a four-top with menus under my arm, I greedily shoveled a huge bite of salad into my mouth.

My first taste of bleu cheese was a revelation, like waking up and realizing that I'd died and gone straight to Hell. It was as if my salad had been tossed with chunks of thick black mildew harvested from damp window molding, or scrapings from a million fetid, bacterial armpits. It was like licking Satan's taint, really getting my tongue into every unbelievably foul nook and cranny, lapping up every diabolical curd. It was so bad I dropped the menus, spat the mouthful of chewed romaine onto the floor, and started crying from the sheer shock of having something so terrible inside me so intimately. I remember the shocked expressions on the faces of my four-top. When I returned from the bathroom to clean up the nasty, chewed mess on the floor, they were gone.

That was my first and only experience with the kind of cheese that features deliberate veins of rot. And writing about it

PAIN

now, I have the uncontrollable urge to go brush my teeth. I swear I can smell the decay on my own breath even now.

Like a fast, rude hand up your skirt on a crowded bus, the bite of bleu-cheese-tainted salad was a hit-and-run assault. It was nobody's fault, really, but thinking of it now, my stomach flutters in outraged revulsion. It's "blue" because it's *rotten*, people. I don't eat maggot-blown meat, either. Blue mold is Nature's Mr. Yuk sticker: It tells us that the food in question is not fit to eat. There isn't enough garlic in the world to change my mind on that.

TO EXPLAIN MY second nonconsensual cheese contact, you'll have to understand that my parents were very young when they had me, and that I grew up in an era when firmness was a central tenet of good parenting. To be unyielding was merely a way to extract cheerful compliance from your child. The experts who wrote best-selling books advised parents to state their demands, then enforce their authority without mercy. So it's not that my child-hood was particularly horrid—it's that in the mid-'70s, *everyone's* was, pretty much.

When I was very young—seven years old, at the most—my sweet Okie father decided that my diet was lacking in a specific dish he deemed nutritious and altogether necessary for my proper development: grilled cheese sandwiches. Ignoring my protests, he slathered a piece of whole wheat bread with mayonnaise, then melted cheddar into the bread. I remember the waxy, rotten smell of the cheese filling the kitchen. I remember my horror and dismay. From babyhood I'd hated cheese—but despite my stated antipathy, my parents persisted in serving it to me. In retrospect, I realize that money was tight and the big five-pound logs of cheese my parents retrieved from the Food Giant were affordable protein, and that, again, they were doing the best they could with very little guidance. In 1978, nobody wanted to raise a picky child.

"Mmm," said my dad. He quartered the piece of cheddared bread with his mayonnaise-smeared butter knife, leaving dollops of grease on the edges of each piece.

"I used to eat this as a boy," he said. "Sometimes we'd melt tuna underneath."

Some of the things he ate as a boy I liked—for instance, mixed together peanut butter and jelly applied to bread in such a manner so that each bite of sandwich contained equal portions of both instead of unincorporated lumps of salty peanut butter and too-sweet Welch's Grape. I liked the cans of pork and beans he'd heat on the stove in a pot too, though I carefully removed the white strips of fat that occasionally polluted my portions. My father had explained that those wormy white ribbons were actually pork, but I'd never seen meat that slimy and pale before. It was better just to lay them on the side of my plate, like the fat my mother pulled off her bacon.

But cheese? *Melted* cheese? I *hated* cheese—I always had.

The smell of the grilled cheese made my mouth water the way it did before I threw up. I couldn't put it in my mouth. I felt weak with loathing. I shook my head decisively, pushing the plate away.

"No," I said.

"You'll sit here," said my young, terrified father. *No tolerance of picky eating,* insisted the TV experts. *Not even once!* "You'll sit here until you eat it."

We sat, my father and I, in a Norman Rockwell semblance

of father-daughter compatibility, separated by a platter of impossible food. At seven, I didn't have the words to tell my father that what he had given me was making me sick and that I could not eat it, and never would—so we sat in silence. I tried not to accidentally inhale the cheddar fumes. The minutes ticked by. My milk warmed to room temperature. I squirmed and whined, kicking my chair savagely.

After an hour my father had finished reading the newspaper, which he'd folded into neat rectangular quarters. "Take two bites," my father said, finally. I shook my head, clamping my nose defiantly in the *Pee-ew!* gesture I'd learned from TV.

We stared at each other. Neither one of us even so much as glanced at the sandwich between us, though the smell of it persisted in nauseating me. My bottom was sore from sitting. The light had changed, too. It was dark outside—past my bedtime, I knew. My father had begun to frighten me. His stony face was unreadable. I missed my laughing, gentle father—who was this stranger?

"One bite," the intruder said flatly, pressing his palms to the table. Clearly, it was his final offer.

Sadly, I considered my options. They were woefully few. If the thing masquerading as my father would not let me leave the table until I ate what it told me to eat, I would have to eat what it gave me. It didn't matter if it was rat poison, iron filings, or a curl of dog shit from the parking strip in front of our house. I had to put it in my mouth and chew it, no matter how much it stank, no matter how nasty it looked. There were no alternatives I could see—to get my father back, I'd have to obey this stranger. My body was the battleground, and clearly, its well-being would have to be sacrificed.

I picked up one of the small, cold squares in front of me. My father-thing was suddenly, hopefully attentive. I felt a spike of hatred that came and went so quickly it was almost not there at all. *You'll be sorry when I'm dead,* I thought. *You'll cry and wish you were dead too.* I pictured myself lying still, hands gracefully folded, in a pretty white coffin. I would be poisoned by the horrible cheese sandwich in front of me, like Snow White with the apple. *She's so beautiful,* people would say. *What a tragedy. If only.*

By that time the cheese had cooled and become opaque with congealed cheese grease, and the smell wasn't so sharp. I kept my teeth away from the mayonnaise. I knew that if that got on my lips or tongue I'd vomit until the Cheerios I'd had for breakfast last Saturday made a second appearance. I nibbled one corner of the quarter, wincing and trying not to inhale through my nose to avoid the garbage-y smell. I was Snow White, brave and doomed. I was being poisoned.

I heaved. *Don't think about it,* I ordered myself. *Don't breathe. One bite—he promised.*

Finally, the half-chewed wad of bread and greased cheese slid down my throat in one gluey mass. My poor father smiled in relief: The experts had been right. It had taken a long time, but I'd obeyed. My *picky eating* had been defeated.

I stared at him, pressing my lips together miserably. *Poisoned.* The rancid, oily texture, the sour taste, the stink of it, like old farts on the hot plastic seats of my father's battered, orange VW Bug. I swallowed, then gagged.

Snakes of vomit shot out of my throat in ropes, pooling in my plate, soaking the rest of the hateful grilled cheese. I retched miserably as my father lunged for the roll of paper towels that hung under one kitchen cupboard, then emptied my stomach again down my own chest. The vomit felt warm and comforting in my lap. Encouraged by the heat, I released my bladder. Hot urine soothed my sore bottom then puddled beneath my chair. Surprised and embarrassed to have wet my big-girl pants like a baby, I burst into tears.

My father cleaned up. As he sopped up my urine with big wads of paper towels and emptied the vomit-drenched grilled cheese into the trash can under the kitchen sink, he wept too. We sobbed in tandem, though my tears were mostly relief to have lived through my poisoning. The stone-faced stranger was gone and the hateful sandwich had been vanquished.

I was just glad to have my father back. Handing him individual paper towels folded neatly into squares, I forgave him with all my heart.

WHEN PEOPLE GIVE me expensive cheeses as hostess gifts, I serve the cheeses immediately (breathing shallowly as I dissect them, it's true) and then slide the leftovers right into the garbage, once my guests have gone home.

In restaurants and at dinner parties, I've learned to feign lactose-intolerance or self-righteous veganism, depending on whether the rest of my meal includes animal parts or not. In a city like Seattle, not a single person questions my dietary strictures. My refusal of cheese goes unchallenged and unquestioned. My *no* always means *no,* and my voice is clear and firm.

Nowadays, when I refuse to put something in my mouth, nobody is ever unwise enough to argue.

BOUNDARY ISSUES

LOAVES
AND FISHES

I FEEL LIKE A FAILURE. LIKE A BIG FAKER.

I'm writing a book primarily about the sensual things I love—food, sex, women's bodies, *my* body—and I'm hungry and scared and broke. These days, the closest I come to gracious living is paging through the glossy lifestyle magazines at my gym. It's like writing a book on travel by looking at pictures of exotic countries on the Internet.

I'm feeling screwed over and sorry for myself, and I'm sick of pretending I'm living simply and elegantly when in reality, my refrigerator is empty, my last meal was boiled potatoes with salt and pepper, and I had to cut the multiple eyes and rotten spots out of the spuds before I could cook them. I'm tired of filling up on what's here. I want to pick at something expensive and savory for a change. I'm writing a book on sex and food, and I haven't been laid in a month and I can't afford groceries.

This strikes me as the blackest of all possible humors.

The tiny paycheck I receive from my part-time word-processing job twice a month was spent a week ago. I'm staring down the barrel of next month's rent and all I can do about that is pray.

I pray that I'll be able to pay for a place to live for another month—that I can somehow make something out of nothing and have a few dollars left over for food, too. For six months I've been a magician: I tap my hat and out springs just enough money to pay a bill—$40 here, $20 there—but at this point, my stage patter's getting old and my trusty hat's as piebald as a mangy old stray. I'm never entirely solvent. My money-fu is more like triage: I just pay the bill that's screaming the loudest or has been ignored the longest.

My laptop is dying.

Please, God, just let me finish this book.

It's amazing how much poor people pray—I find myself doing it constantly. Apparently poor people have God on speed-dial. All I know is that I'm praying, praying, praying, and my prayers used to be for things like an end to global misogyny and a renewed interest in solar power, and now I'm praying *Please, God, let cut-up fryers still be on sale for $1 a pound* and *Please, God, let me be a good enough creative writer to finish this book without anyone knowing I've been eating Top Ramen for a week straight.*

God's probably sick of my constant calling—I don't blame Him for letting His machine pick up instead. *Your call is very important to Us.* I know He's lying, but I stay on the line and leave piteous little messages anyway.

I FEEL LIKE my poverty is really testing the thesis of this book—that everyone has a right to good food, *no matter what.* "No matter what" means no matter if the Y key is sticking or if I haven't paid my electric bill in full since last spring. "No matter what" means no excuses—even in the thickest midst of my poverty and depression I have to find a way to give myself good, nourishing food. Because if I don't, who will? And if I don't, how can I prove that I love myself enough to make changes in an untenable situation? And how will I attain the energy or will to make those changes?

I think the whole idea hinges on sifting out the things you can actually control.

Because Lord knows I can't control this fucking Y key, and I can't control next month's rent, and I've got a two-inch reverse skunk stripe of Crazy Lady black roots on my dyed-blond hair that I can't afford to control either, so you know I'm not at what you might call, My Personal Best.

But:

If my dinner tonight is more boiled potatoes, well, so be it. Potatoes kept my Irish ancestors alive for generations—I guess they're good enough for my pale Irish ass. Throw some cheap whiskey on top of those potatoes, and you've got a two-course meal. Pare a few onions into the potato-boiling water, and you've got your salad course. How fancy do you want to get, anyway?

I can either eat those potatoes and hate them and feel angry and miserable and screwed, or I can eat the potatoes and do my best to taste what's delicious about them, and let them nourish me, and be thankful for them. Either way I'm probably supping on potatoes. The only difference is what side dish I choose: Self-pity is certainly one choice, but the better one might possibly be a little

PAIN

humility. Because as bad as things are, at least I'm eating *something*. And my laptop's still mostly working, despite the wonky Y key.

I shouldn't be using so many adverbs anyway. My verbs need to toughen up and start pulling their own weight. We all have to pitch in these days.

IT TURNS OUT that tonight for dinner I'm having a can of tuna and a piece of bread. Tuna was on sale and the bread was cheap. Tuna for protein and bread for bulk—it's not cut-up fryers for a buck a pound, but it's better than another package of salt-flavored noodles.

I think it's easy to live a lush life when you have every resource at your fingertips. But maybe part of what I'm supposed to be writing about is taking pleasure in the small things that are easy to overlook—like a simple dinner, eaten alone, in a peaceful apartment. Maybe my craving for rich food and luxury has been so loud that I've missed the small, quiet voice of appreciation for what I do have.

So tonight I'll put my fish dinner on a bright, pretty plate. I'll toast the bread. I'll fix myself a glass of water, with ice cubes and a straw. I'll add freshly ground pepper to my tuna and maybe drizzle some olive oil and balsamic vinegar on the top to add depth of flavor. I'll sit at my kitchen table with a good book. And I will deliberately enjoy every bite of my meal, noticing and appreciating every nuance of flavor, aroma, and texture. I will pretend I've never had tuna and bread before in my life, and I'm trying to write an essay describing my delicious meal for *Gourmet* magazine. I will insist upon pleasure, because if that's the only thing I can control, I want as much of it as I can get.

I'm going to try something else after dinner, too: I'm going to speed-dial God and when His machine clicks on, I'm just going to say *Thanks*. I figure He might appreciate hearing something besides *It's not fair* and *Why can't I have* and *Please, just kill me now*. You gotta keep 'em guessing, even when they're omnipotent—He only gave us free will to see what kind of crazy shit we'd be up to, and I, for one, hate to disappoint.

PAIN

HEARTBREAK 1: WHEN YOU CAN'T STAND TO EAT

MY HEART IS BROKEN. I THINK I ACTUALLY HEARD IT CRACK.

It sounded like a wishbone: a dry snap. When I was growing up and my mom roasted chicken for dinner, my brother and I would set the wishbone on the kitchen windowsill to parch. After a few days, giggling, we'd make wishes and pull it apart. Whoever got the bigger half of the bone got his or her wish. I usually wished that boys would like me, or that I'd wake up one morning to find myself miraculously slim and beautiful and popular.

Unfortunately, I stayed toadish and unlovable through high school no matter how many roast chickens my mom made. I watched other teens date on TV, marveling at the handsome boys who drove cars and wore khaki pants and actually asked girls out to restaurants and movies, paying for them and casually holding their coats over one arm. I wasn't even jealous: It was like watching African tribal mating rituals on the Discovery Channel, as unreal and fascinating as science fiction.

Now that I live alone, I don't bother to save and dry my wishbones. Who would I break them with, anyway? That would be like thumb-wrestling myself—half of me would win, the other half would lose. Those odds aren't exactly inspiring. So now I just throw my bones away—it's better to be without wishes than to be a constant half-loser.

MY HEART BROKE a few nights ago while I was trying to find the gentle, sensible phrases that would keep my man from walking out on me.

We'd had an argument. It escalated. I knew he was tired and hungry. I thought that if I made us a meal and he slept over that night, we could resolve our spat in the morning. He, on the other hand, was angrily packing his belongings into the plastic grocery sacks he retrieved from the cabinet beneath my sink. *He knows where everything is in my apartment,* I thought. *Doesn't that mean something?*

In my hesitation and misplaced pride, desperately tongue-tied, I waited too long to speak and the moment passed me by. It was over. He grabbed his coat and slammed the door behind him—just like in the movies. It was very confusing—it had all happened so fast! One moment I was a girlfriend . . . then all of a sudden, I wasn't.

Can he just do that? I wondered. *I mean . . . really?*

The answer shot back immediately: *Not only* can *he, sister—he* just did.

230

PAIN

I scanned the apartment frantically. He'd left his coffee press and a pile of books! That had to mean something, that he'd be back—didn't it?

But before I could even indulge myself in a moment of optimism, Negativity arrived on the scene like an ambulance-chasing lawyer. *Nope!* came the first response, delivered in a tone so positive it was almost gleeful.

He's done with you, another voice added savagely. I imagined a hateful old woman pressing her lips together and nodding her head—*Done with you, slut!*

I was only distracted momentarily by the sound of his car starting outside before hearing a discreet interior *pop!* It sounded like a nonmicrowaveable plate undone by the rigors of low-grade kitchen radiation: a tiny explosion in a plastic box. My heart—the fist-size muscle that I'd always imagined as ruby red and robust—had turned out to be as brittle as an old chicken bone left too long on a kitchen windowsill.

Instead of wishing and half-losing, I'd held back and lost everything.

Now there are shards and mess everywhere. I find fragments of broken plate and bone in every bite of food I try to swallow. They stick in my throat and make me bleed.

I'M LOOKING ON the bright side, trying to be a half-winner for once.

If the diet pill industry could bottle the appetite-reducing power of heartbreak, every obese person in America would be stick-thin—even skinless chicken breasts and steamed vegetables don't melt weight off as quickly as misery. I can rub the knobs of my own hip bones above my belt. Unfortunately, my face appears mummified from all the crying. A few times I've woken up in the morning with dried-blood tracks running from my tear ducts all the way to my jaw line. I can't explain them except to posit that it's a miracle, like a weeping statue of the Virgin Mary.

I suppose the blood could be from the broken blood vessels around my eyes. Each tiny hemorrhage calls attention to the brand-new under-eye bags I'm suddenly sporting. For the first time in my life, I look my age.

In the mirror I am dismayed to see the hateful old woman who told me my man wouldn't be back, and every day her mouth gets tighter and meaner. Her skin is dry and flaky, like piecrust. When I blink sadly, she blinks. Her eyelids are scaly and reptilian. She is a wicked thing—chewing on hair and splinters, spitting out rat poison. *Nobody loves you, whore,* she says merrily, just for the mean fun of it. When I cry her eyes glisten like wet rocks.

I AM OFFICIALLY *care-worn,* like the Velveteen Rabbit. I am missing one button eye, and my velveteen fur is matted and worn away in spots. My stuffing is coming out in clumps, and there is nobody who wants to love me, not a single person to stitch me up and brush me off and make me their own soft, huggable possession again. My best days are behind me. I'm ugly as sin, greasy, discarded. I'm like those sad stuffed animals in pediatricians' waiting rooms—handled cavalierly by many but not good enough to belong to anyone. I can only distract the querulously sick and, even so, my extremities bear the vicious bite marks of frustration. I have been chewed ragged.

I DON'T EAT for two days. On the third day, I have two beers and an entire frozen pepperoni pizza for dinner. The grease gives me a stomachache, and after half the pizza I don't even want any more, but I make myself finish it anyway as punishment for giving in to my hunger.

I resolve to do better. Starvation feels like the corporeal manifestation of heartbreak, and when I am physically weak and dizzy, it is a relief to wear my pain on the outside. All of a sudden I think I understand the people who cut themselves, forcing their pain into a visible, quantifiable state. Razor slashes and hunger are like controlled burns: They take the pressure off an unworkable system. And when you are desperately hurt, substituting another kind of hurt can feel like relief.

IT'S BEEN THREE weeks since my door slammed shut, sealing me into my sad little apartment with my new roommate, Negativity. Negativity doesn't have a job and never goes out, so we've been spending a lot of time really getting to know each other. We both like *Flavor of Love* on VH1. Negativity has pointed out to me repeatedly that no matter how awful the ladies on the show are, they're still more loved and desired than I am.

I breakfast on a handful of multivitamins then ride the bus to the gym, where I run on the treadmill until I'm panting for breath. For the first time in my life I am without appetite—food holds absolutely no interest for me. I am light, I am lifted. As my brain chemistry shifts from the endorphins being released by my workout, I feel good for the first time in days. Food has nothing to do with it! Who needs food?

I drink water from my bottle and feel pure, blameless. I can live through the next few months if I can just maintain this feeling. I need it—it's my heroin and I am high, sailing above pain like a dove. At the same time I realize that the good feeling is about as real as the weaves worn by the *Flavor of Love* ladies, and underneath that light, lifting sensation, I'm losing my mind with sorrow and self-loathing.

I add another hour to my time on the treadmill anyway. My plan is to run until I'm too tired to feel anything at all.

While I run, I imagine the following scenario: My lover calls me up, says he needs to see me—he can't stand to be apart from me, he can't stand the separation. I allow him to come to my apartment, where candles are burning and I just happen to be wearing my tightest pants and a skimpy tank top, both of which are loose on my suddenly tiny frame. I am physically vulnerable. I am *little*.

Seeing me so small (and yes, I am barefoot—I mentally add movie star red toenail polish, though I haven't had a pedicure in months), my errant lover sweeps me up in his arms, lifting me effortlessly.

"My God," he says. "You're so *thin*. I can feel every bone in your rib cage!"

(Wait—actually, instead of *rib cage*, how about *spine*? *Rib cage* reminds me of poultry—split breasts sheathed in Saran Wrap on little plastic trays, with tiny meat maxi pads beneath to sop up the blood and fluid. Poultry is not what I want to be thinking about. Yes, *spine* is definitely better.)

"My God," he says. "You're so *thin*." (That's my favorite part right there.) "You're so *thin*. I can feel every bone in your spine!"

I smile bravely. I have wasted away like a Victorian heroine without the nourishment of his love, locked away and forgotten in a dusty attic. I could have died without ever uttering a single word of reproach or complaint.

"God, Sarah, I missed you so much!" he says, burying his face into the intersection between my bony shoulder and my willowy, swanlike neck. Then he lifts me into his arms and carries me to bed, where he carefully undresses me, revealing my delicate frame.

Mentally I add white, lacy underthings. I am innocent. I am tiny. I am a tiny, innocent victim of love. I starved without his affection, drooping like a lily when he took the light of his love away. *That* is how much I love him—I am an ethereal being; I live on affection and batten on kisses.

Then he fucks me and I come during missionary position instead of afterward with him using his hands. Somehow my lacy underthings are still in place, undisturbed and unsullied.

I nest in his arms peacefully, feeling protected and adored.

My toenails still look great.

THEN THE FANTASY is over, and I snap out of it, and I know that this is *complete bullshit*.

Starving myself will not bring my lover back.

The solace it offers is fake and venomous, like ugly razor scars on inner arms. Starving is not my friend. Starving does not want me to feel better. Starvation wants me to continue feeling shitty about myself. Starvation knows that the hungrier I get, the less ability I have to analyze, to explain, to *think*. And if I'm not doing those things, starvation can stay curled up like a snake against my *rib cage*. Telling me lies. Making me do its dirty work.

That lifted, light feeling? That's from exercising—not from starving. And if I starve, I can't exercise. That's just simple math without a single x or y variable—and even though I failed algebra twice, I can still add and subtract.

I cannot punish or atone this pain away. I have to walk through it. It's all mine—nobody else can come with me. Anesthetizing the pain away by mainlining hunger will not get me through. I cannot be a coward. I do not have that luxury.

My heart? Broken, sure, but there's nothing wrong with my brain, and my brain says, *Knock that anorexic shit right off, lady, and eat some fucking food. You need all your energy to figure out how to stay alive right now.* And you know what? My brain is right, I do.

I step off the treadmill. It's time to go home and eat.

I START WITH FRUIT.

A cup of frozen raspberries. A cup of plain, whole-milk yogurt. Half a cup of water. Two scoops of wheat bran. Into my blender it all goes.

Now I have a fruit smoothie. I pour it from the blender into my special Guinness pint glass. I add a straw. I am suddenly ravenous.

As I suck down cool delicious raspberry slush I take back everything bad I've ever said about raspberries. For a while I'd gotten so pro-strawberry I'd forgotten all about raspberries—they seemed played out, overused, ubiquitous. For a long time strawberries just seemed nicer to me—more traditional, more complex and subtle, more *adult*—whereas raspberries were flashy and mainstream, kid stuff.

But this smoothie is blowing my mind because it tastes like real raspberries, and the creamy yogurt is a perfect foil for their sharpness and sweetness. It's like my palate is waking up again after a long period of being battered by a diet of frozen pizzas and pills and tap water and sadness. These raspberries are *perfect*. I'm gulping them down in big greedy swigs, my straw pushed to one side of the glass.

Raspberries, I'm sorry I ever disrespected you. You are so good. I was wrong.

After finishing my smoothie I take my blender apart and clean each piece with warm sudsy water. While screwing the crown of blades back into the base of the glass pitcher, I'm thinking about one thing:

Cooking. For one. For me.

HEARTBREAK 2: SUSTENANCE

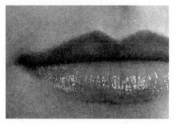

I'M ALONE. I'M WALKING AROUND MY APARTMENT PICKING things up and putting them back down again. Nothing I pick up or put down makes me feel less alone. Some days are harder than others. Today is Mount Everest. It is an effort to breathe.

I open the fridge and see four tall, cool bottles of beer. They're so cold, each bottle sparkles with precipitation. They look so much like a beer commercial that I am half-tempted to don a bikini. They are ridiculously inviting. I want to stand in front of the open refrigerator and drink them all down, one after another. It is ten o'clock in the morning.

Breathe.

I close the refrigerator door.

I open it again.

Hello, beautiful! sing the bottles of beer in a tinkly chorus. *Why don't you just drink us? We love you! We don't want you to feel lonely!* It's so nice to have friends again that I almost accept their invitation.

The only thing stopping me is the promise I made to myself yesterday after the gym—to call off the desperate self-sabotage, and cook something for myself. I can't afford a midmorning beer stupor. As lovely as it would be to stand in front of the refrigerator gulping down my frosty friends one after the other, I have to cook.

THIS IS ABOUT staying alive when your whole body is telling you to go back to bed, pull up the covers, and sleep until you're dead.

First, go to the store and buy yourself one of those big containers of mixed organic salad greens. Throw a handful of greens on a plate and drizzle them with the store-bought dressing of your choice. Magically, the leaves morph into salad and voilà, you're eating your vegetables. Do this once or twice a day.

Try draining a can of tuna and dumping that onto the greens before adding the salad dressing. Now you're not only eating your veggies, you've also added a big chunk of protein. See? Not hard.

Reduce your expectations—don't expect food to cheer you up right now. It won't. But eat it anyway. Keep eating.

Buy some fresh fruit—apples, oranges, bananas, whatever. Get a mix if you like. Take the fruit home. Wash it, dry it, and put it in a bowl on your table or kitchen counter. Eat a piece once a day or so. It's already been washed and dried so it's zero effort. All you have to do is eat one piece and you're done.

This is life support. This will keep you alive until your heart mends enough to keep you out of bed and away from midmorning booze-a-thons. This will help you put one foot in front of the other, plodding forward, breathing the thin air of Mount Everest and staying sane enough to know that sometimes a girl's just gotta cry, and it doesn't mean she's losing her mind—it just means she's sad. So *be* sad.

But cook while you're crying. That way you'll have a hearty meal all ready to go after you finish blowing your nose for the umpteenth time.

BLACK BEANS AND RICE

Put about two or three cups of dried black beans into a large-ish pot. They will sound like ball bearings when you pour them in. This may or may not amuse you.

Cover them with water, up to a couple inches above bean level. You can always add more water as you go. Turn the range heat to high until the water starts boiling, then cover the pot and reduce the heat to low so the bean-water is simmering in a relaxed, nonurgent way.

Don't salt the beans yet or they'll stay hard. You want the beans to soak in the simmering water, softening from ball bearings into squishy little pellets of carbohydrate-y goodness. If you have some, toss in a few bay leaves.

The softening process will take several hours.

Check on the simmering beans every now and again, and add more water if needed. Stir them with a wooden spoon to make sure the beans aren't adhering to the bottom of the pot. They probably won't be, but I'm a compulsive stirrer and you may be too, so indulge yourself and stir that damn pot to your heart's content.

After a few hours, test the softness of the beans by squishing one against the side of the pot with your wooden spoon. If it squishes easily, they're soft enough.

Take the cover off the pot and turn the heat up a little bit. Now you're boiling off any excess bean-soaking water that may be in the pot. You want the beans moist and soupy, but not watery. (Stick your face over the bean pot and steam your pores while you're at it. Your poor skin could probably use some relief.)

Here are some things to throw into the pot while you're adjusting the liquid. Pick a couple, or all of them, or include other ingredients that aren't on the list but seem like they might be tasty to you. Remember that black beans aren't exactly packed with flavor on their own, but because they're neutral and starchy they carry other, stronger flavors very well. Think of them as plain bread—a culinary tabula rasa, an efficient vehicle for deliciousness as opposed to being delicious by themselves. Now's your chance to make your beans taste like whatever you want them to taste like. Knock yourself out!

- A handful of chopped onions.

- Salt to taste. "Salt to taste" means a lot of salt if you're a salt-hound like myself—just keep tasting and adding more until the beans seem right to you. You can use seasoning salt or kosher salt or sea salt or flavored salt of any kind. You can use soy sauce but don't use the low-sodium kind, because the whole point of soy sauce is to increase the salinity of your beans. Salt gets a pretty bad rap these days and if you have massive hypertension you may wish to avoid using a bunch of it, but salt is a reliable flavor enhancer that amps subtle taste up to a scrumptious 11, so do use some. Salt is my friend and I would like it to be yours, too.

- A glug of olive oil or a small chunk of butter or a spoonful of bacon fat. Not a lot—maybe a tablespoon's worth, maybe a little more, maybe a little less—again, "to taste." Fat helps to make your beans filling and satisfying to your palate.

- Some diced-up bell peppers. Red, yellow, green, purple, it doesn't matter. They all have their charms. I just buy whatever's on sale.

- A glug or two of vinegar—balsamic, red wine, apple cider, or whatever you have. Vinegar goes really well with fat—the two ingredients bring out the best in each other, setting each other off and creating a third savory flavor composed of the best elements of both. Think of fat as the daddy and vinegar as the mommy. They love each other so much they have a baby. And the baby tastes delicious!

- Ground black pepper or cayenne pepper, though if you're using cayenne add it in small increments because a little of that goes a long, mouth-burning way.

- Leftover chunks of cooked ham, bacon, chicken, or sausage. You know how I feel about sausage by now. You should really have it in your kitchen as a staple.

If you don't (or if, God forbid, you're a vegetarian) just forgo the meat and realize that vegetarian food will simply never be as tasty as nonvegetarian food, and that's just the way it is. When us meat-eaters are dying of colon cancer and looking back on all the fine meaty meals we consumed in our lifetimes, you can interrupt our bacon-laced reveries and tell us you told us so. Until then, I'm buying family packs of chorizo and putting it into pretty much everything I cook that isn't birthday cake.

- Spices. Oregano and cumin are nice. Maybe some chili powder. Or—and especially if you added sausage—try a little fennel.

Once you've got your bean-liquid adjusted and your stuff added, turn the heat down as low as it goes, cover the pot, and let your beans sit. The longer they sit, the more flavor emerges from the extra ingredients you added. Long, slow cooking also results in a smoother, creamier texture for your beans.

Now make a pot of rice. If you have a rice cooker, follow the instructions. If you don't, dump two cups of rinsed white rice into a pot and add three cups of water, or chicken broth if you want to be fancy. Heat the pot on high until the water boils. Let it boil for a minute or two, then turn the heat down as low as it goes, put the lid on, and set your timer for twenty-five minutes. Fluff it up with a fork and let it sit on the burner uncovered for a few minutes if it still seems a little wet. Sprinkle it with salt and pepper if you like, or leave it naked.

Take a big-ass bowl and put a bunch of rice in the bottom of it. Then use a ladle or a measuring cup to scoop up your beautiful black beans and deposit them over the rice. The black bean juice will soak down into the rice, giving it wonderful bean-flavor, and the beans will kind of sit on top looking scrumptious and half-mashed. If you didn't add enough salt while the beans were stewing, sprinkle some on top of them now before you devour them (last chance!). Watch for bay leaves if you used them. Don't accidentally eat one. They taste bitter and soapy—I know this because I've eaten my share, unfortunately.

You can make a black-beans-and-rice sundae if you want! Spoon salsa over the top like hot fudge, then add a few dollops of sour cream or plain whole-milk yogurt for the whipped cream. If you're a pork-lovin' fool like me, you can then crumble a handful of crisp bacon over the top of your sundae for crushed nuts. The jimmies, should you feel that no sundae can be complete without waxy little pellets of dye and food-grade wax, can be dried parsley flakes or freshly ground black pepper. The cherry on top's up to you: an olive? A few strips of raw red pepper? Well, if you're me, the cherry on top is probably a Louisiana hot link. But, you know, do what you think best.

If it's not ten in the morning, have a cold beer along with your beans and rice. Like salt, beer is known to be a very effective flavor enhancer.

Remember that if your beans don't come out as flavor-packed as you would like—in other words, if despite all the ingredients you've added and all the times you've taste-tested your beans as they cooked, adjusting the spices and salt accordingly, and your beans *still* seem bland to you—Tabasco sauce is your friend. Mellow green or classic red, chipotle or smoked, or whatever other sales gimmicks they can devise. It doesn't matter—it's up to you. But Tabasco sauce, and lots of it. There's a reason all bachelors have bottles of it in their otherwise-empty refrigerators.

Tabasco sauce will also scour out your sinuses if you consume enough of it. And if you're congested from off-and-on weeping, this can feel very, very good.

You'll have leftovers for days, and if you wrap your cold black beans in a tortilla, you have a to-go meal. Take your homemade burrito to a park and eat it. You don't have to talk to anyone or share your meal with the squirrels or do anything but scowl at pigeons and eat your delicious black bean burrito. Remember, this is life support.

You are winning.

HEARTBREAK 3: COMFORT

HE CALLED THIS MORNING.

The phone sounded very loud and jangly in my empty apartment. It scared me. I realized my phone hadn't rung in days, nor had I spoken to anyone except the checkers at the Safeway two blocks from my apartment. When I'd presented my Advantage card my voice had come out in a croak, and I'd had to clear my throat in order to be understood. Since that trip to the grocery store, though, my prepubescent boy's voice hadn't been a problem. I hadn't spoken with anyone in four days.

When I heard his voice on the answering machine I dropped the carton of Ben & Jerry's I was having for breakfast and scrambled for the handset.

Why can't you just love me? I wanted to demand. *Why can't you come home? Why can't this be easy?*

"I hope you're well," I said instead, sounding as stiff as a brand-new dress shirt, cardboard collar points still intact. *I miss you so much* is what I meant. *I can't stop thinking of you. Everything in my apartment reminds me of you. I think I'm losing my fucking mind.*

"I'm fine," he said. "I hope *you're* well." His voice sounded similarly starched, like he was reading from a script called *The Two Most Boring People in the World Have a Stilted Conversation.* This was madness.

I wanted to scream. We were Heckle and Jeckle, the two overly polite cartoon crows. If we kept waiting for the other one to go through the doorway first ("No, after *you!*"), we were never going to get anywhere. And yet I couldn't stop being courteous, speaking to my lover as if we hadn't shared entire nights wrapped in each other's bodies, glued together with sweat and come, sleeping only to wake and devour each other all over again.

Please love me the way you used to. I never stopped loving you.

"Getting any painting done?" I inquired.

"Some," he said. "And how's your writing going?"

Horrible. Fucking shitty. I can't write. I hurt too bad to eat. Please come home.

"Great!" I said. "Thanks for asking!"

"Glad to hear it," he said.

I suddenly wondered if he was lying about his painting the way I was lying about my writing. Were his brushes dry or caked with crusted paint, tossed down in frustration? Was he being tortured by blank canvases the way I was being tortured by empty pages and false starts? Did he wake up every morning in dread of more wasted hours, more time in which his art was *not* being created?

Was he eating ice cream for breakfast and watching the *Flavor of Love* marathon on VH1?

Why were we lying to each other?

"Well," I said.

"Nice to talk with you," he said.

"Yes," I agreed. *Last chance!* Say *something! Anything!*

But instead we just said goodbye, replacing our respective handsets into their cradles softly, as if cautious not to offend.

THE MOST TEDIOUS thing in the world is heartbreak. Not in the acute, not when it actually occurs—not in the moment when you hear a small dry *pop!* inside your rib cage and think of chicken bones and microwaved plates. That's kind of exciting, if only because it's so definitive—and if you've been around the block a time or two, you learn that that *pop!* means you're pretty much fucked for the next couple of months. Clear your schedule, hold your calls, and make sure you're current on your cable bill even if your gas bill has to wait, because Lord knows that late-night TV's gonna feel like your only friend for a good long time. That's what you get when your heart implodes. A lot goes on in that one tiny moment! If it weren't so annihilating it would probably be a little beautiful, like a diamond cut into hundreds of perfect facets.

But heartbreak as a chronic condition is a long, slow trudge.

I, for one, am sick of it, no matter how many cartons of ice cream I allow myself to have for breakfast. I'm still losing weight, though I couldn't care less about turning into the delicate tiny-boned creature who starred in my fantasies of romantic reprieve a month ago. My body's on autopilot, rudderless without

PAIN

appetite, and no amount of ice cream seems to be making much difference—but as long as I'm eating something filling at least twice a day and kicking ass at the gym, I'm fine with that. I finished the last of my black beans two days ago. I'm farting cumin and Chubby Hubby.

Also, I'm fucking horny as hell. I'm my own ravenous demonlover: I don't care if my ass smells like a spice rack dipped in fudge and peanut butter. I can't keep my hands off myself. My heart may be frozen, but my cunt didn't get the memo. She's red-hot and purring like a Detroit muscle car. I've worn out two packages of C batteries, killed my old faithful Slim-Line vibrator dead, and melted the finish off my brand-new Rabbit Pearl knock-off. I'm as insatiable as a porn star, except that I'm having real orgasms and my own are rarely pretty, more like grunting muscle spasms than photogenic bliss. *I want I want I want I want,* my body says. It won't shut up. And it's not like I have a normal job. I can drop everything and rape myself every ten minutes if I want to. I can stop in the middle of a sentence and return to it while I'm still breathing hard, my fingers slick on the plastic keyboard of my laptop, and nobody's the wiser.

And even though I'm technically having a nice time, I suspect that part of my sudden surge of self-lovin' is just me looking for a way to feel a little bit cared for, to make up for the fact that I'm no longer being touched and held at all. I am my own Wire Mother: a frame of metal covered in a thin towel, offering cold comfort. My joyless diddling is only solace projected through a scrim of eroticism. I know this, but I don't know what else to do.

I don't bother putting on high heels for myself. I'm an easy lover, though admittedly, I lack passion. I know all my own best moves by heart.

TUNA NOODLE CASSEROLE

You may or may not have grown up eating Tuna Noodle Casserole. I didn't. Some of my friends did, though, and now they either love it or hate it. There isn't much ambivalence possible in a dish nearly synonymous with Mom and Home, whether or not your childhood actually included good memories of either thing.[1] Tuna Noodle Casserole is classic comfort food and after a vicious breakup, you need all the comfort you can get.

There're all kinds of ways to fancy this up, but I'm gonna give you the wham-bam version, and you can tart it up however you like.

First, boil and drain a package of pasta according to the directions on the bag or box—not the spaghetti kind though. Use rotini, elbow macaroni, the little sea-shell-shaped ones, bowties, or even flat egg noodles—basically anything bite-size and compact, not long and strandy. Rinse the cooked pasta with cold water. This gets the excess starch off your noodles so your casserole doesn't get gluey. Set aside.[2]

Now get a big-ass mixing bowl and dump in a can of Campbell's Cream of Mushroom soup. (Avoid the low-sodium/low-fat

---

1. If you want to know what my childhood tasted like, it's Swanson's Salisbury Steak TV dinners and Campbell's Vegetarian Vegetable soup. It's not that my mom couldn't cook, or was a lazy homemaker. I just loved TV dinners and canned soup and clamored for them constantly, and every so often my mother would relent and allow me to have them instead of more-nutritious fare.

2. And, for what it's worth, I love reading recipes that say "set aside," as if we're so dim-witted we have to be reminded to *physically move a bowl or ingredient out of the way* so we can concentrate on the next part of the dish. Like, "Oh my God, I've mixed the dry ingredients and now I need to mix the wet ingredients, but I *can't*, because the dry ones are *still in the way! WHAT DO I DO NOW???*"

kind, of course—*yecch*. Taking away the salt and fat from a can of cream soup leaves what, chemicals and binding agents? Pass.) Fill the can halfway up with milk, and throw that into the bowl. Open and drain two or three cans of tuna, and use a fork to add those to the milk and soup in the bowl. Add about half a package of frozen peas. Use a spoon or fork to kind of mush everything together (and yes, at this point it *will* resemble a pile of frat-boy vomit—this changes, I promise, but if you're cooking for a finicky eater it's probably best to send him or her to the store on a fabricated mission right about now, lest your casserole languish uneaten later). Dump the drained, rinsed pasta into the mixing bowl and mix until the noodles are evenly coated with the soup/tuna/pea mixture.

Now get a baking pan—9 x 12 is good. Coat it lightly with nonstick spray (or rub a little oil in it to keep your casserole from sticking), and turn the pasta mixture into the pan. Sprinkle grated parmesan over the top. Bake at 375°F for about half an hour, or until the cheese appears nicely browned and appetizing.

Now, here's the thing: You can use Cream of Anything soup instead of Mushroom. Cream of Celery is actually very nice if you don't mind your casserole appearing slightly corpse-green under strong light.

You can add frozen broccoli florets instead of peas.

You can use leftover cooked chicken or turkey cubes instead of canned tuna. If you do, try using Cream of Chicken soup for a variation.

For that matter, you could use a few cups of diced ham instead of tuna. (I'd recommend sticking with Cream of Mushroom soup for that, though, not Cream of Celery or Broccoli. Nobody likes cadaverous ham except Doctor Seuss.)

You can add more grated parmesan to the soup/tuna/noodle mixture before you turn it into the pan, if you really like parmesan. Or you can sprinkle mozzarella over the top of the casserole, or romano, or pretty much any other white cheese you think would be good.

You can add dried or fresh onions. You can add parsley. You can add black pepper. You can add a pinch of nutmeg to the soup/milk mixture. Seriously, nutmeg's good—it brings out the creaminess of the soup and acts as an accent for the tuna flavor. But don't use more than a smallish pinch—a little nutmeg goes a long way.

If you're feeling extra-fancy, you can mash up potato chips and sprinkle them over the top of your casserole before baking. Some Southerners wouldn't dream of making Tuna Noodle Casserole without crushed potato chips, claiming the whole point of the dish is to act as a vehicle for its own crispy, salty, fried topping.

One last thing: You know those cans of fried onion bits that you only buy around Thanksgiving? If you happen to have any of those, throw 'em on top with the parmesan and the chips. They're so good! But I never have any on hand because when I buy them I just end up eating them straight out of the can with my fingers the second I get home, like movie popcorn.

For dessert, make:

BERRY COBBLER

This recipe is my own variation on something I got from *Southern Living*. I tricked it out a little bit, but I bow down to *Southern Living*, because even though it has a lot of crappy old-lady articles

PAIN

on gardening and decorating, it also features a lot of excellent, nonfussy recipes using seasonal ingredients.

This recipe is sound as a motherfucker and will simply never, ever fail you. I make this for guests all the time because it's easy and scrumptious. People love having fruity things for dessert because despite all the sugar and butter that combine to form the backbone of any good baked dessert recipe, most folks consider fruit "healthy." I mean, it's just *fruit,* right?

1 C white sugar

⅔ C white flour

⅓ C cornmeal

1½ t baking powder

½ t salt

½ C butter, melted (½ C = 1 stick, just FYI)

2 C frozen berries (I've made this with raspberries, blackberries, strawberries—even blueberries! So use whatever berry you like best)

Mix the dry ingredients together. Pour in the melted butter and whisk till just blended—you're not trying to get all the lumps out. Pour batter into a lightly greased square baking pan (I use my 8 x 8 or 9 x 9). In a separate bowl, sprinkle your berries with 1/4 C white sugar and toss them until they're pretty much coated. Then drop the berries *over* the batter and bake at 350°F for about seventy minutes, or until the top of your cobbler is golden brown and you're half-nuts from the delicious baking smell of it. (Note: the berries sink into the batter and end up at the bottom of the dish by the time it's done baking.)

Serve in bowls with scoops of good vanilla ice cream all melty on top. Sprinkle the ice cream with a little cinnamon if you like, just to be fancy. Eat with a spoon.

Berry Cobbler is also really good reheated for breakfast when you're tired of having ice cream by itself. What's healthier than fruit for breakfast, I ask you?

AFTER YOU EAT your Tuna Noodle Casserole and your Fruit Cobbler, take a bath and put yourself to bed. Sometimes you have to be your own good mama and let yourself be comforted.

Good night, Sleepyhead.

HEARTBREAK 4: SUMMER BERRIES

SUMMER IS WANING. MY BIRTHDAY CAME AND WENT. I baked myself a chocolate Betty Crocker cake to celebrate and frosted it with canned vanilla icing that was so sweet it made my teeth ache. I decorated the cake with fresh sliced strawberries that I eventually picked off and ate by themselves.

I'm thirty-six now. Thirty-six feels exactly like thirty-five, but I like that my age is now divisible into three equal twelve-year chunks. Three is the magic number, isn't it? Zero to twelve, twelve to twenty-four, twenty-four to now. So far I think I like the last chunk best. You couldn't pay me enough to live through the middle chunk again.

I've been thinking about Home a lot lately—what makes a Home? Who's responsible for it? Is Home something you can have by yourself, or do you need a family to have one? Is just staying in your apartment alone on Friday night enough to make a home a Home? Or is Home just another word for *community*—the wolf pack of people you love and spend your time with, in all their messy and constantly changing permutations of singleness and parenthood and partnership?

At thirty-six I'm an Old Maid. I've never been married. I stay home, earning my living by putting words on paper. I cook for myself, freeze things to eat later, and make sure that what I consume is as fresh and delicious as it can be. I preserve, occasionally. I'm learning to bake my own bread. I even own a second-hand couch that I stretch out on when I read. Having a couch is just as great as I'd always thought it would be.

But do I have a Home? Does all my cooking give my apartment a warm core? Am I the beating heart of my own residence?

Can I be a homemaker, even if I live alone?

I've never wanted a traditional marriage: the big white dress, the beaming parents, the catered dinner for 150 guests, the awkward formalwear. But all externals aside, I've never met the person I knew, without a doubt, I would stay with for the rest of my life. I don't believe in divorce and I don't believe in affairs, so to me getting married means knowing damn sure that out of all the people in the entire world, you'll be able to stay in love with—and faithful to—one person. But then again, maybe my idealism's inoculated me against actual marriage the way a porn habit creates chronic dissatisfaction with one's real-life partners. Maybe if I didn't believe so strongly in monogamy, I'd have the opportunity to test my theories on it. All I know is that for ten years, most of the clients who jerked off in front of me wore wedding rings—and if that's their idea of marriage, give me my spinsterhood. I may be alone, but at least I'm not being betrayed by someone who's pledged to love and honor me forever, forsaking all others.

Despite my previous career providing sexual entertainment to strangers for money—or perhaps, because of it—it's clear to me that erotic intimacy was designed to nourish our hearts and keep us close to each other. Subverting that by using people as objects wounds us all. If there's anything I've learned it's that love is an unstoppable human drive, fierce and universal, and that sex is the physical manifestation of love. And that sex without love is missing the whole damn point. Sex brings us home to love.

It's all so clear to me now that I'm alone. And now, no matter how much I try to make my apartment feel like a warm, safe nest, I feel like the heart of my home has been yanked out, whole and throbbing, and tossed aside as offal.

A FEW DAYS ago I bought a half-flat of fresh blueberries off the back of a pickup truck at the local farmers market. They're bruised and pulpy and startlingly sweet, tasting of sun and earth and green growing things. The blueberries are the best things I've eaten in weeks—straight out of their boxes, chilled from my refrigerator. I try to remember to wash them before I eat them, but gluttony and impatience win far more often than I'd like to admit. I'm sure I'm becoming sterile from the pesticides.

But still. I'm making blueberry buckle and blueberry betty and blueberry crumble. I'm making blueberry-bran muffins and blueberry-sour cream coffee cake. I'm contemplating a cold summer soup, thick with heavy cream and pureed blueberries. I'm gobbling handfuls of them, plain and unadorned, staining my fingers and my keyboard with winey purple splotches. This morning, my shit was blue.

The phone rings as I'm popping blueberries into my mouth, one by one. I swallow, and pick up the handset. "Hello?"

"Hi," he says. We both freeze. *What's next? Who says what?*

Oh honey, I miss you. Please come home. I'm biting my lip. I want him so badly. The sound of his voice on the phone has raised the tiny blond hairs on my forearms, like a magnet raising iron filings. He is my magnet, pulling me to him even when he doesn't want me.

"What's going on?" he asks, like we talk every day and this particular phone call is no big deal.

"I'm cooking," I say. I'm lying. But I'm not about to admit to standing in front of an open refrigerator chomping on pesticide-laced berries, fetchingly attired in big white comfort-panties and the same Slayer T-shirt I've been wearing for three days.

"So, I was wondering . . . " his voice trails off.

"Come home," I say.

"What?"

"Please come home." I am crying. It's terrifying to say the words. I hate saying them. What if he laughs at me? Or simply, kindly, refuses?

"I have a kitchen full of blueberry breads and muffins and cobblers that nobody's eating," I say in a rush. "And I can make us coffee. You left your press."

Silence. I can hear him thinking, considering.

COME HOME. I have never wanted anything this bad in my entire life. *COME. HOME.*

"I'll be over in an hour," he finally says.

WHEN HE ARRIVES, he has a plastic grocery sack in his hands. He's so handsome I can't breathe. I can smell his skin and his summer-day sweat. I feel faint. I feel like vomiting. The air between us is vibrating lightly, sizzling like a plucked guitar string. Every cell in my body is drawn to him. I'm a shaky unbathed mess with dirty feet and snarled hair. I am not in my tightest pants nor a skimpy tank top. I'm not tiny. There are no lit candles. This is not how I pictured our reunion at all.

We don't smile at each other. I move back into my apartment, and he follows. He puts the grocery sack on my kitchen table silently, then sits. I busy myself by opening the bag to put the contents away, bustling as if under deadline. I still can't look at him. I am humiliated by my stubbly legs and my sour breath. Why, why, why hadn't I showered first, or at least swabbed my crotch and pits with a warm washcloth? I'd been so surprised when he'd said he was coming; half of me didn't believe he would actually show up.

Half of me doesn't believe he's sitting in my kitchen right now. It's possible that I've lost my mind and am hallucinating out of sheer need. I consider pinching myself hard. But what would that prove? Crazy people can pinch themselves as hard as they like and they still need their Depakote. It's not like craziness is a dream from which you can wake. Being nuts is like being broken-hearted: Asleep or awake, you're pretty much doomed to a version of reality that's not what you'd like it to be.

He shifts in his chair and tries to look into my face, but I'm keeping my eyes down, focused on the task of unpacking this bag. *Nope! Not ready yet!* My cheeks feel hot. I must look ridiculous, like a red-faced tomato on scissoring legs.

Was this a bad idea? Did I fuck everything up by asking him to come over? I am miserable. He probably doesn't even want to be here. He probably already has a new girlfriend, someone prettier and cooler and nicer than me. All of a sudden I feel a crippling wave of shame. *How could I have done this? Humiliated myself?*

But to my astonishment the grocery bag contains the makings of a hearty breakfast for two: a dozen eggs, some bread, a pint of half-and-half . . . and a package of hickory-smoked, thick-cut bacon. The bacon sits between us on the kitchen table like a gun. It is the elephant in the room. Neither of us look at it.

I finally meet his gaze. It's the scariest thing I've ever done in my life. His face is kind and open and sad. I have every inch of it memorized, but it's still a revelation.

I love you, I think. Then, *Can we please take care of each other?*

ALL THE THINKING I've been doing about Home, home-making, family—nothing has prepared me for the realization that this really is my life, and it's half-over, and it looks like I'm never going to be the cheery mom baking cookies in my own clean, spacious kitchen while my partner works and looks forward to coming home to a hot dinner. In reality, there are no children and I live in three small rooms by myself, and most months I have no idea how I'm going to pay the next month's rent. I've crisscrossed the country a hundred times, like blown dandelion seed, staying on threadbare couches with well-meaning strangers, washing quickly in public restrooms, hustling meals and cash and shelter with the pragmatic efficiency born of necessity. Nobody's ever going to mistake me for a mother or a wife or the kind of person who buys furniture or owns the place I live. I've made a thousand grievous mistakes, broken hearts, and treated people unkindly when they deserved compassion. I was a *fille de joie* and now I'm a writer, and either way, I've chosen to walk a path that's both solitary and uncertain.

But Home is what you make of it, I guess. The best some of us can do is to camp out in rented rooms and make small, true alliances with each other. When we eat together—when we fuck each other—for those tiny moments, we're not alone, and Home seems like something we can hold on to and keep forever. We can taste it, feel it on our skins and inside us; it lifts us up and gives us a reason to stay alive one more sad, lonely day. And that's not what I wanted when I was a child dreaming of a home and a family of my own, but it's going to have to be enough, because that's all some of us get. And I'm grateful for every meal shared and every intimacy—every sweet, crazy burst of connection. If that's all we get, then I will love every single moment I'm allotted, fiercely and with my whole dumb, hopeful heart.

I LOOK AT the groceries spread out before me and consider the breakfast I'm going to make tomorrow morning. Bacon and eggs and many hot cups of coffee tempered with cream and sugar. Maybe blueberry pancakes. My mouth is watering. I can practically taste every bite, every sip, from the smoky crunch of crisp bacon to the sugarcane sweetness of the coffee. I'll cook a leisurely meal after Beau and I wake up together. We'll eat it and then maybe fuck again, and that will be enough to keep my heart beating until the next tiny moment of grace.

And just for a moment, thinking about the meal I will cook for the person I love, I can almost touch and taste Home—I can almost *see* it, shimmering in the distance like a gorgeous, beckoning mirage.

It is the most beautiful thing I know.

AFTERWORD (CHERRY ON TOP)

I'VE BEEN WATCHING MY CARBS FOR THE PAST WEEK TO SLIM down for my author's photograph.

My first author's pic was pretty hot (if you don't notice the fact that in my hurry to smile pretty for the camera, I'd completely neglected to brush my hair), so now the stakes are high. The last thing I want is for haters to pick up my second book, flip to the back, and smile in disbelief and pity at my Dorian Gray–like transformation. So I'm watching my carbs and curbing my booze intake because it seems like the older I get, the more my face puffs up like an airbag the day after I overindulge.

I admit it: I'm vain. I'm pretty sure that most writers are, because if we weren't, we wouldn't detain you for three hundred pages, clutching your lapel and breathing whiskey fumes into your face as we insist upon telling you our Very Important Stories. We grew up being encouraged to express ourselves by well-meaning parents and a lifetime supply of gold stars from English teachers, and now as adults we blithely assume the right to hijack people's attention. We spend our days contemplating the complexity of our own navels (and then painstakingly *documenting the process* of our own inward gaze), so you'll have to excuse me for being a little concerned about my author's picture.

Oh yeah—we also tend to be control freaks.

I guess if you've made it all the way to the Afterword you've probably spent a fair amount of time reading my book, and for that I sincerely thank you. Here are some things you should know about the book you just read:

1. My editress, Brooke Warner, is an immortal godlike superhero-creature of unerring instinct and endless patience. The good parts of this book are a direct result of her stunning ability to dissect vibrant text from unnecessary bloviation. (That's right, I'm a bloviator. Where's my telethon?) The sucky parts of this book are my fault, and represent the times I've sulkily scrawled STET in the margins of her perfectly reasonable edits.

Miss B., this book couldn't have been written without you. You're as much its mommy as I am. You're the Good Mommy who makes school lunches and sews Halloween costumes from scratch, and I'm the Bad Mommy who naps in the middle of the day, has hangovers, and wears a Wonderbra to Parents' Night. But as everyone knows, it takes two mommies to . . . well, I guess it doesn't take two mommies. But if you're lucky, you get two, and if you're *really* lucky, one will be as sweet, practical, and tactful as Miss Warner.

264

2. This book could also not have been written without the love, support, financial assistance, and treats given to me by the people I am proud to call my friends, both online and meat-realm. You've fed me, entertained me, let me cry and snot all over your dry-clean-only shirts, and, most of all, you haven't punched me in the face for my nonstop, single-minded focus on THE BOOK THE BOOK THE BOOK THE BOOK for the year it's taken me to bust this out. I honestly can't believe I still have friends. But I am so damn grateful that I do. Thank you for tolerating me, my dearly beloveds.

3. If you're curious about what's going on with me, you can read my online diary at www.sarahkatherinelewis.com. Never a fee, and worth every penny! Swing by and say howdy, especially if you have a good recipe to share or want to pay me a lot of money for my writing.

4. All right, I'm just going to do this. I don't know where else to put this and I really want this recipe to be in my book, because it is *so absurdly good*. It is also very low-carb, if you plan to wear plastic pants in your author's picture.

PUMPKIN SOUP

Cut up a few shallots and sauté them in a tablespoon of butter or bacon fat in a big pot over medium-high heat until they're soft, but not caramelized.

Add two 14-ounce cans of chicken stock and one 15-ounce can of pumpkin. *Do not* fuck up and use canned pumpkin pie mix instead. Seriously. Just the normal canned pumpkin is what you want here.

Add 1/2 teaspoon ground black pepper, 1/4 teaspoon cayenne

pepper, and 1/2 cup dry sherry. Bring the mixture to a boil, then reduce the heat to low, cover the pot, and simmer for half an hour.

After half an hour, remove the pot from the range and stick it in your fridge. Allow your soup to cool until it's no hotter than lukewarm, then run it through your blender or food processor in batches until smooth (this doesn't take long since everything should be all soft and cooked already—you're just making sure the shallots are pureed into the rest of the pumpkin mixture so they're not lumpy and weird and distracting in your mouth when you're finally eating your soup).

Return the blended soup to its pot and add 1 cup of heavy whipping cream. Don't be a baby and add milk instead in an effort to make this recipe low-fat, because the texture will be all wrong—you want heavy whipping cream and nothing but. (Remember, *fat is your friend*. Cream just wants to be your buddy. Don't snub cream—that's mean. Reach out to cream. If you don't, who will?)

Add a splash more sherry and a generous pinch of nutmeg. Add more pepper if you want a spicier soup. Add a little salt if you screwed up and bought the reduced-sodium chicken stock that looks so much like the regular kind (bastards).

Cover the pot and heat your soup on medium-low, stirring often. Don't let it boil.

Serve garnished with crumbled bacon bits, of course. The maple-flavored kind gives a really nice autumnal flavor to this soup, but any bacon will do. If you don't have any bacon, you can sprinkle a little nutmeg on top instead, but come on: Why wouldn't you have bacon on hand? It's a staple!

Eat and enjoy.

AFTERWORD

5. Finally, I want to thank the ladies and gentlemen who've shared my bed, eaten my food, and put up with my crap: I didn't deserve any of you, and I hope you know by now that you could've done a lot better. But thank you for gracing me with your time and affection anyway.

And if I've played fast and loose with chronology, quotations, and the details of particular events that you recall differently than I describe in this book, remember that all writers are crazy, drunken liars and you're much better off dating someone with a 401k.

666. SLAYER RULES OK.

7. In all seriousness, a note about the sex industry: Dudes, don't mess with porn. Don't go to strip clubs, don't rent dirty movies, and don't jack off to nasty pics on the Internet. Don't pay for domination, get lap dances, get "massages," or rent women to watch you spank it. That shit will fuck you up—it's addictive nonsense designed to wreck your chances of having loving relationships with real, live females and to make sure that you keep paying for the fake stuff.

Take the money you were going to spend on a month's subscription to a corny adult website with the same tired images you've seen ten zillion times before and ask a smart, pretty girl out. I swear to you that hanging out with an actual female is much more fun than paying for the privilege of becoming just another john. Remember that the sex industry objectifies you just as much as it objectifies its performers. Unsubscribe!

8. Thank you again for reading my book. I hope it made you hungry, made you laugh, grossed you out, and got you hot.

ABOUT
THE AUTHOR

© MARY PAYNTER SHERWIN

SARAH KATHERINE LEWIS is the author of *Indecent: How I Make It and Fake It as a Girl for Hire* and has contributed to several anthologies, including *Fucking Daphne: Mostly True Stories and Fictions* (Seal, 2008). A ten-year veteran of the adult industry in Seattle, Portland, and New Orleans, she now spends her time maintaining her website www.sarahkatherinelewis.com, writing, and playing with food in Seattle, Washington. An outspoken (and often outrageous) feminist activist, she works to promote global revolution and dreams of a world where all women feast like Vikings.